Moonshine

Moonshine

Illicit Spirits in the Appalachian Hills of Rural Southern Ohio

by

Marilyn Thornton Schraff

Copyright © 2011 by Marilyn Thornton Schraff

ALL RIGHTS RESERVED

No portion of this publication may be reproduced, stored in any electronic system, or transmitted in any form or by any means, electronic, mechanical, photocopy, recording, or otherwise, without written permission from the author. Brief quotations may be used in literary reviews.

Unless otherwise indicated, all Scripture quotations are taken from the King James Version of the Holy Bible.

Cover design by Marilyn Thornton Schraff

Cover photo of Michal Thompson by:
Jerry Uhl Photography in Lancaster, Ohio

Library of Congress Control Number: 2011915263
ISBN: 978-0-9827983-1-7

Edited by: Judy Fox
Includes bibliographical references, index of persons and index of illustrations.

FOR INFORMATION CONTACT:
mschraff@roadrunner.com

Published in Cleveland, Ohio, USA
by
Marilyn Thornton Schraff

Manufactured in the United States of America

Also by Marilyn Thornton Schraff

Appalachian Childhood

Memories of Growing Up in Rural Southern Ohio During The Mid 20th Century

To my daughters:

Michal Jasmin and Malissa Jean

Acknowledgments

I would like to thank each of the following for making much of this book possible by assisting in research, providing photographs, extending permission to print copyrighted material and contributing information: Kathy Delawder Akers; Bob Birchfield; David Blankenship; Maxine Bennett Bowman; Michael Caldwell, editor of the Ironton Tribune; Jennifer Chapman of the Ironton Tribune; Phyllis Humphrey Christian; Phyllis Waugh Clary; Ron Davis; John Delawder, Jim Delong; Marcella Dickess Delong; Cora Yates Doyle; Lyndall Murdock Eubanks; June Feuillerat of the Delaware County Genealogical Society; Betty Fradd; Betty Moore Fraley; Dennis Hankins; Daniel Hieronimus; Norman Humphrey; Betty Jenkins; Homer Eugene Jenkins; Paul Johnson; Ricky Johnson; Lori Kersey of the Ironton Tribune; Danny Kitts; Paula Penotte Kitts; Donald Lambert; Randall Lambert; Steven Lambert; Patricia Yates Leeper; Charles Legg; Sharon McIntyre Lightner; Dianna Yates Little; Arthur Main; Dorothy Lawless Malone; George Malone; Charles (Butch) Massie; Bonnie Weber McGoron; Emmett McIntyre; Danny McKnight; Lenora Miller; Olan Mills Studios; Malissa Thompson Nazir; Marta Sutton Ramey of Briggs Lawrence County Library; Carl Ratliff and Mavis Siders Ratliff; Joyce Hardy Roach; Wayne Rucker; George Sanders; Anita Sanders Scherer; Fred Schraff; George Scott; Michal Thompson Searls; Ron Searls; Lori Shafer of Briggs Lawrence County Library; Brenda Moore Spears; Ted Sprouse; Yvonne Yates Strehle; Donald Thacker; Cora Waugh Thomas; Ronald and Viola Adkins Thomas; Jerry Uhl of Jerry Uhl

Photography in Lancaster, Ohio; Harley Vanmeter; James Volgares; Gene Waugh; George Waugh; Evan Walden; Betty Jenkins Walls; Loretta Gail Neal Webb; Sandy Wicker of the Delaware County Historical Society; David Wickline; Peggy Penotte Williams; Mildred Wilson; William Winters of the Lawrence County Sheriff's Department; Forrest Ray Yates; Harold Yates; and Martha Kimble Yates.

I am especially grateful to my dear friend, Judy Fox. She not only contended with the long hours of many weeks spent laboriously editing, then reediting corrections, due to my dyslexia, but was also remarkable in dealing with my (oral and written) rural Appalachian dialect. Her efforts to make *Moonshine* a better read are greatly appreciated.

Table of Contents

Introduction		xiii
Chapter 1	Miss Moonshine	1
Chapter 2	Four Generations of Daughters	13
Chapter 3	A Little History	27
Chapter 4	The Family Manufacturing Business	41
Chapter 5	Business Partners	56
Chapter 6	Revenuers and Lawmen	77
Chapter 7	Federal Court Proceedings	96
Chapter 8	Commentary on Court Proceedings	109
Chapter 9	Other Manufacturers	123
Chapter 10	Culture, Cooks and Chemistry	145
Chapter 11	Remedies and Recipes	166
Conclusion		181

Bibliography	185
Poem: Family Business	194
Index of Persons	195
Index of Illustrations	203
Mail Order Pages	207 & 208

Introduction

After reading my book entitled *Appalachian Childhood,* several folks expressed interest in the little I wrote about my mother's family being in the moonshine business. Their questions, comments, and encouragement are the reasons I decided to write this book.

Moonshine, though always illegal in Ohio, was and continues to be a recognized part of its Appalachian culture. There are moonshine festivals, moonshine pageants, moonshine recipes, moonshine makers, and moonshine drinkers. Moonshining is celebrated in numerous ways including: paintings, music, dance, festivals, movies, books, parades and online.

If a person wants moonshine today, it's easy enough to find. Moonshine is part of hill folklore and a part of Ohio and American history. It is a part of the character, the independence and self-reliance found in a determined people who are proud of their roots. The makers are looked upon as heroes and the traditions are kept alive from generation to generation.

In the Lawrence County Ohio Memorial Day Parade, the longest continuously running Memorial Day Parade in the United States, one can see numerous signs of the cultural significance of moonshine in the area. Moonshining is actually commemorated.

The purpose of this book is to provide information to familiarize the reader with illicit distillation of whisky in rural southern Ohio from Prohibition through the present, including the involvement of my family.

There were several families along the country road where I grew up who made and sold moonshine for a living. There were several more families who made and sold it who attended my grade school and high school. Some even attended our churches. There were also families whose breadwinners made their living as law officers and their jobs were to catch the people who made the stuff. There were some families who didn't make it, but bought and drank it. There were some who discussed it, but didn't make or drink it. There were some who didn't discuss it, but made and/or drank it. There were some who made it and sold it, but didn't drink it. Had it been legal, there were probably more who would have made it. Seemingly every family was involved in one way or the other, some in multiple ways. Some still are.

Aside from the distillation business, moonshiners and bootleggers were (are) no different than other folks. They went to our schools, helped their neighbors, fought in wars to defend our freedoms, married, raised and supported their families, and died. Some never got caught, so folks didn't know as much about their business. Some were arrested and served jail time or prison sentences. Some were caught and received suspended sentences or were placed on probation. Some discussed it openly. Some didn't even discuss it with their children.

It is neither my intention to praise criminal behavior, nor is it to condemn or judge anyone for the way he or she chose or chooses to support his or her family. I'm merely presenting some data to inform the reader.

In *The King James Version of the Holy Bible* in St. Matthew, chapter seven, verse one, Jesus says, "Judge not, that ye be not judged."

Except for the anecdotal contributions, the information that follows is documented and verified by multiple sources. It is about my family, our neighbors, community and culture. Hopefully you will find reading it informative, entertaining and enjoyable.

N.B.

My spelling preference of "whisky" over "whiskey" will be used consistently in this publication, except when "whiskey" is part of a quotation. "Whisky", according to Wikipedia, is the modern preferred worldwide spelling of the word.

Chapter 1

Miss Moonshine

In the spring of 1988, while living in Logan, Hocking County, Ohio, I read an article in *The Logan Daily* about an upcoming festival and pageant in a nearby town, New Straitsville, in Perry County. The article had a form for young women from Athens, Perry and Hocking Counties to enter as contestants in the Miss Moonshine Pageant.

As I read, I thought about my beautiful teenage daughter, Michal, and how she lacked the self-esteem she had as a younger child. Perhaps every mother thinks her daughters are beautiful, intelligent, poised, talented, sweet and kind, but I knew mine were far above average in every way.

Michal Jasmin Thompson was born December 19, 1971, prematurely by approximately six weeks. From the first moment I saw her, I knew she was my little princess, a blessing from God. Prior to her birth, I had chosen the name Laurel Jasmin for the child I was carrying, should it be a girl. However, upon first sight of her, she was so perfect and so beautiful, I knew she needed a royal name. Thus I choose one from my favorite Bible story of Saul and David. King Saul's daughter was Princess Michal and she became the bride of the next King of Israel, David, son of Jesse. My little, newborn princess was named Michal Jasmin Thompson.

My husband thought it only fair for him to name our next daughter. He chose the name of Malissa Jean against my wishes, as I wanted to name her Merab Jeanette, after

Princess Michal's sister (I Samuel 14:49) and my older sister, Janet.

My little princess and me in 1973

Both of my daughters did well in school, in sports, in music, artistically and in dance. They were interested in God and religion. Their faith was an inspiration to me.
Michal had battled some birth defects, but (with faith and the help of Children's Hospital in Columbus, Ohio) was determined to overcome. Malissa's hyperactivity was her

challenge and mine, but she learned to use it in a positive manner. The two of them were my princesses, my pair of aces, my reasons for living.

Michal and Malissa Thompson
with braided hair in 1981
(Photo printed with permission from
Olan Mills Studios)

Like pieces of a jigsaw puzzle, my daughters were a perfect fit, complimented one another and made our home very happy. Each morning for many years I French braided their hair as we prepared for school and work. They looked like live baby dolls, filled our house with laughter and were in numerous activities. They were full of energy and beamed with love. Both were self-assured and esteemed by their peers.

By eighth grade Michal was over six feet tall and had a fine figure. She was asked by the owners of a small clothing chain to model in their spring style show in a neighboring city, Lancaster. It was a wonderful experience for her and broadened her interests. She took more pride in her appearance and learned to style her own hair. Without the braids, she no longer looked like a child. She was maturing into a delightful young lady.

When school was out for the summer of Michal's eighth grade year, both girls were together running errands to prepare for a camping trip while I was at work. While on those errands, Michal became the victim of a violent crime. It was a traumatic time for her. Malissa took good care of her older sister when I had to be at the office. It was a sad time for all of us.

Hospitals, doctors' offices and courtrooms seemed to take over our lives. Michal became introverted and withdrawn. She didn't feel good about herself anymore. To me she was prettier than any Barbie doll, but she didn't see herself as I saw her.

As I read the requirements for the pageant entrants, I knew within my heart I had a winner. My daughter had many talents. She could sing. She could dance. She was beautiful. She was a mother's dream come true.

Michal had already completed the Red Cross Swimming Program and obtained her first job with the State of Ohio as a lifeguard at Lake Logan, part of the Hocking Hills State Park. She was to start Memorial Day. Getting the job pleased her, but didn't quite bring her back to her previous high on life. I wanted her to be happy again.

According to the information in the newspaper, The Moonshine Festival was Memorial Weekend. The Miss Moonshine Contest would be prior to the festival, so would not interfere with Michal's first job.

I gave it some thought, then filled out the contest entry form without even consulting my daughter, because she was so modest she would never have considered entering any kind of pageant. I thought the competition would be good for her and hoped winning would restore her self-image. I was confident she would win.

When I did tell Michal about the entry form and my sending it in, she was not pleased with me. She thought an older girl from a more prestigious family would win and that she did not stand a chance. I did a good job of convincing her it would be fun, that she'd make some new friends and that Malissa and I would enjoy being her cheering section.

Because young women from three counties were eligible for entry, there were many competitors. I trusted the judges would be fair. With that and knowing my daughter, in my mind, it was a win-win situation.

We had been to previous Moonshine Festivals. The parades were long, but entertaining. There was a genuine still, and it actually produced moonshine. There were rides, games and food booths with moonshine burgers and moonshine pie. There were musicians and other forms of entertainment each year. While living in Logan, we went together as a family and had an enjoyable time. My daughters always saw other children they knew from school, 4-H, Rainbow Girls, church activities, sports, swim classes, or dance lessons.

Moonshining is a part of our Appalachian culture. Even the *Appalachian Encyclopedia* mentions the Moonshine Festival. However, it is in error because it states the festival is in Hocking County instead of Perry County. The festival in New Straitsville, Ohio, has been around for more than 40 years, beginning in 1970.

It was fun for the three of us to prepare Michal for the contest. We made some changes to a gown we purchased for her to wear in the formal competition. She had been given a couple of outfits from the store owner who had her model and one was perfect for the song and dance routine all the girls performed together. The excitement of her first job and the activities with the Miss Moonshine Contest put some zest back into my daughter.

Yet, although she was having fun, Michal did not feel she had a chance of ever becoming Miss Moonshine. I remember my becoming upset with a fellow standing next to me during the pageant, as he warned me to be prepared to deal with the heartbreak of losing once the runner-ups had been announced and the anticipation of the proclaiming of the winner heightened. Not one time did losing ever enter my mind. However, with so much silence in the crowd, it seemed a long time before the queen was named.

Michal won! Her smile was radiant. Malissa and I were delighted. That instant was the beginning of Michal's restoration of self-esteem. She was a winner! She was more than just my princess. She was the Moonshine Festival

Queen. She was the ambassador for travel and tourism for the Hocking Valley Area. She had chaperones (Kenny Burgess, Rema Brown, and Bonnie Butler) everywhere she went and was truly treated like royalty.

During her reign, she was in parades from Lake Erie to Winter Haven, Florida. Her photograph was in store windows and newspapers. She was on stage with TV stars. She was happy again. Her self-image was improved.

Tom Wopat, actor, (Luke Duke from the Dukes of Hazzard) and Michal Thompson, Miss Moonshine, in 1989

Michal at age 16
beginning her reign as Miss Moonshine
(Photograph printed with permission from Jerry Uhl)

I will never forget my mother's comments of pride in Michal's new title of "Miss Moonshine". It was more than her just being a proud grandma.

Michal Jasmin Thompson
Miss Moonshine 1988

She said, "Mommy would really be pleased to know there was an official Moonshine Queen in her family. Mom was so proud of Michal's title, I made arrangements for her and my sister Shirley to fly to the Citrus Festival in Winter Haven, Florida, with me just to see her in the parade. Michal traveled by car with her chaperones and had several other stops along the East Coast before arriving in Florida.

We all had a wonderful trip.

My sister Shirley Comer and Mom from Ironton, Ohio, and Bruce Johnson from South Bloomingville, Ohio, are standing along the Citrus Parade route waiting to see the Miss Moonshine from Logan, Ohio.

Rema Brown, Bonnie Butler, Kenny Burgess and Miss Moonshine, Michal Jasmin Thompson, at a parade

At the time, I never fully understood Mom's pride in the Miss Moonshine title, or why Grandma would be so pleased, even though Mom brought it up numerous times. I thought it was just a few words of a proud grandmother. However, I knew my daughters would make any mother or grandmother proud and never gave her comments a lot of thought until after I started research for my first book.

If only I had known more of my family's history, I could have appreciated Mom's pride in Michal's new title and how it all connected with my mother, Grandma and my uncles. Now that I do understand, I want to share our family's story, an important part of America's heritage and of our Appalachian culture.

Yes, I am a proud mother, a patriotic American and am honored to be a product of my Appalachian culture and the family that shaped my children and me into the successful women we are today.

A beautiful, happy Miss Moonshine

Chapter 2

Four Generations of Daughters

My maternal grandmother, Cora Alice Delawder Yates, told me about her life growing up. Born November 13, 1889, she was the only surviving daughter of Joseph Delawder and Lydia Alice Neal Delawder. She attended school with my paternal grandfather, Martin Thomas Thornton, and some of his siblings. Aside from school, her only other social contact was attending church. At home she helped take care of her younger brothers, did ironing, milked cows, sewed, embroidered and helped with the housework, cooking, canning, churning and soapmaking. Being the only girl with seven brothers made lots of daily chores, including washing dishes, making beds, changing and washing diapers and other laundry. She also had to help carry water, firewood, ashes, and assist with the gardening. Grandma told me that at seventeen she decided if she were going to have to take care of babies and do so much housework, that she could at least get married, have her own home and babies and be her own boss. She told me she chose to marry Grandpa because he was so handsome, and because his family had more money than hers. Grandpa was eight years older than Grandma, and she felt he was mature and ready to take on a wife.

My grandmother never told me about any love or romance, or how she met Grandpa. Just this past year, I learned my maternal grandparents were second cousins via the Neal family. Grandpa's mother was Polly Ann Neal and his father was Isaac Yates. So, I now believe Cora and

Walter knew each other long before their marriage because they were kin, as Lydia Neal Delawder was Grandma's mother.

The above photo is of Cora Delawder Yates and Walter Neal Yates on their wedding day, December 24, 1906. She was 17 and he was 25.

Through the years, one or two of Grandma's brothers lived with her and her children, as Grandpa, a stonemason, worked away from home most of the time. Grandpa's brother, Great-uncle Ike Yates, and his wife, Nellie, lived in the nearest house to Grandma and Grandpa. Grandma was addressed several ways: Mommy or Mom by her children, Aunt Corie, and Miss Yates by most folks outside the family. Mom's siblings called Grandpa "Poppy".

Although I never knew Grandpa, I knew from the first time I met Grandma that she was kind and loving. She provided me with much encouragement, praise and loving memories. Her cheerful attitude and sense of humor made her a delightful person.

Grandma and Grandpa lived well in a prospering, fast-growing industrial country. My mother, Vedna May Yates, was born to Walter Neal Yates and Cora Alice Delawder Yates on September 9, 1923, the youngest of eight children. One child, Shirley, had died in infancy, leaving seven surviving.

According to court records, Grandma and Grandpa married on December 24, 1906, and divorced in March of 1926. Although Grandpa had sued her first, his suit was denied. The divorce was granted to Grandma on the grounds of Grandpa's abusive behavior toward her and the children.

Grandma was awarded full custody of the seven children, nearly two hundred acres of their jointly owned real estate, and the home on Elkins Creek, a part of Aid Township in Lawrence County, Ohio. The final settlement contained no means of support or other financial provisions for Grandma and her minor children.

Earl Randolph Yates was their oldest child. He was born October 9, 1907. Marion Rosco was born October 21,

1910. Edna, Mom's only surviving sister, was born December 17, 1911. Forrest Rose was born May 13, 1913. Shirley Marie Yates was born February 6, 1914, but never survived her first year. Isaac Orlyn Yates was born January 25,1918. Joseph Pearl Yates was born March 11, 1920, and Mom, Vedna May Yates, was born September 9, 1923.

Earl, their oldest child, was eighteen at the time of the actual divorce. According to information Grandma passed on to me verbally, Uncle Earl had been diagnosed with a severe heart condition as a teen and doctors had advised her that he was not able to do physical labor.

Grandma took the doctors seriously and so did Uncle Earl. I never knew of him to work a day in his life. If he ever did, it was a well-kept family secret. However, he was occasionally required to do a few chores, like feed the chickens or bring in buckets of water and coal, or take out ashes.

As stated in my previous book, Grandma was the most concerned person I have ever known about the safety and well-being of children. There was no way she was going to risk Uncle Earl's health by making him work. When she was old, I remember her asking him to take out ashes or bring in coal, and he would put his hands over his heart and complain of chest pain. I often thought his chest pains were faked to get out of work. Grandma loved him anyway and not only tolerated his laziness, but provided him a home and took care of him until 1964, the year she died.

In addition to Uncle Earl's health condition, Grandma had another special needs child who required constant care. Uncle Joe was disabled from childhood with a severe condition of epilepsy and had numerous grand mal seizures all of his life. One seizure caused him to fall into a burning fireplace and left him with many scars. He was self-conscious because of them and would rarely let anyone take a photograph of him.

Uncle Joe Yates

Grandma told me that because of Uncle Joe's fall into the fireplace, she closed it up and never used it again. There was not going to be another chance for a child to be injured at a fireplace in her home. She then bought a coal/wood heating stove and had it installed in what she called her dining room. That stove was the main source of heat in the Yates home for the rest of her remaining days.

The other sons were helpful and hard workers. They helped farm Grandma's land, raised crops, cattle, pigs, chickens, and worked for others picking corn, hoeing, plowing, or whatever they could find to do to help support the family. Aunt Edna was not there to help with the housework or to tend to the other children, as she left before the divorce was final. Mom was too small at the time to be of any assistance to the rest of the family. Uncle Earl studied law and helped tend to the younger children while Grandma worked in the fields with her healthy sons.

Grandma sold her cream
in cans like the one above.

Grandma sold eggs to Hannan's Grocery Store and cream in the old metal milk cans to a man who picked them up from her back porch. I remember him coming to pick up the cans, but don't remember his name. Her big blue cream separator was kept on that porch near a large, round, oak table with a red and white checked tablecloth where she washed and placed her eggs in cartons for sale. Grandma was still selling eggs and cream when I was a child. Sometimes I think about Sunday dinners with my siblings and cousins on her screened back porch near the old cream separator and it always brings back fond memories.

Aunt Edna seems to have been a daddy's girl. When Grandpa left Grandma, Aunt Edna did too. Grandpa paid to have her boarded in Aid so she could finish high school. Her children are the only grandchildren who have memories of Grandpa. He died at Aunt Edna's house in 1942, long before I was born.

Edna Yates as a teen

According to Wikipedia, in October of 1929, the United States stock market crashed, beginning the Great Depression. In 1930 there was a severe drought in the agricultural heartland of the United States. This impaired farming and other agriculturally related areas of employment. In 1931 a deflationary spiral started. By 1933, world trade reached bottom. Farming, logging and mining jobs plunged. Unemployment was high in those fields and there were few other jobs.

West Virginia documents verify Grandpa married again in 1931, but Grandma never remarried. She was an industrious, determined woman, full of love and energy. It still pleases me today to hear so many people compliment her. She was positive, pleasant and praised by those who knew her well and by those who have provided information to me.

Mom's sister, Edna, was the only one of Grandma's children to have completed high school. Her children have told me Grandpa paid her way through nursing school in Columbus, until she married Uncle Ed.

Grandpa's diary has an entry with no date as, "Miss Edna Yates 664 N. Park St. Columbus, O, % Henderson Hall," which somewhat substantiates the fact that she attended school in Columbus.

Thus Grandma remained single and provided for herself, five sons, and my mother without the assistance or support of Grandpa, or the aid of her oldest daughter, during the greatest depression our country has ever known.

There are some legal documents to indicate Grandma's brother, Hobart Delawder, lived in my grandmother's home and helped with a manufacturing business Grandma and her sons operated together.

Several people have informed me that some of Grandma's brothers were in the same business and assisted their only sister and her dependent children in getting their business up and running.

I have written a whole book about my Appalachian childhood, so will not go into much detail about my generation. I will say that it was after World War II, that we worked hard and that our country was growing and prospering. I was born December 12, 1947, the third and middle child of William Luther Thornton and Vedna May Yates Thornton.

My children, Michal and Malissa, and Mom had some things in common. They were all raised by a single mother, one who had to work to provide for them with little, or no support from their fathers. All were beautiful, had siblings, and were loved very much. Each had one sister, but Mom did have several brothers. I was fortunate to have completed a college education and supported my family by teaching school and as a counselor/social worker. Mom's mother was not as fortunate in that respect, but prospered well with what she did have.

Mom's youth was relatively different. She did not have the conveniences of running water or a bathroom. She did not complete high school or have dance lessons, music lessons, swimming lessons, fine doctors, or have the privilege of knowing any of her grandparents. Yet she talked about a happy childhood, felt loved and was well provided for financially via the family manufacturing business. As an older teen, Mom had to use rationing stamps to make purchases. Neither my children, my grandchildren, nor I have ever had to deal with government rationing.

Michal and Malissa were raised during the most prosperous times in American history. My mother grew up during the worst times, yet she never complained. She knew Grandma loved her and did the best she could under the conditions to which she was subjected. Grandma was a survivor, a heroine to her children, grandchildren and to many of those who knew her.

Mom often compared the upbringing of my daughters to her own, as she could relate to what it was like growing up without a father in the home.

She would tell my daughters, "You can't miss what you've never had."

Vedna May Yates Thornton at 17

Shown in the photo above from the viewer's left to right are: Marilyn (17), Shirley (11) and Janet (20) Thornton on Marilyn's graduation day in 1965.

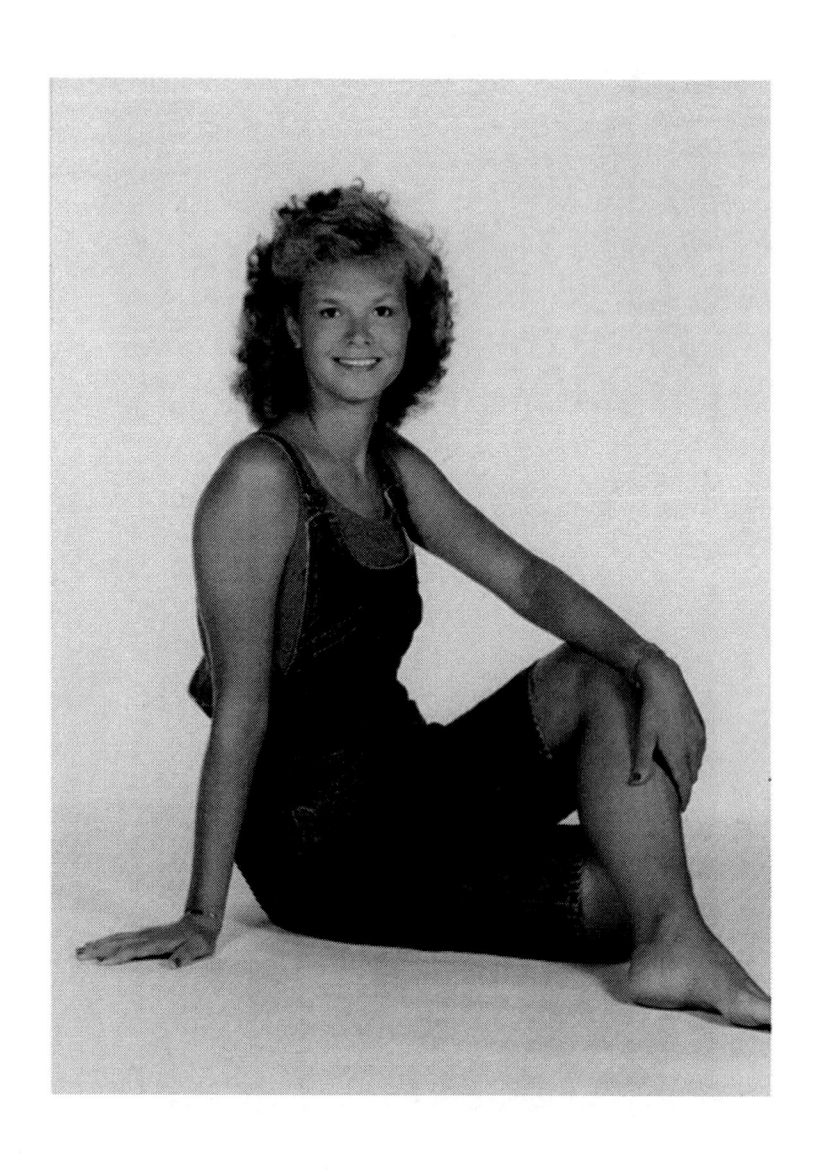

Michal Thompson as a teen
(Photograph printed with permission from Jerry Uhl)

Malissa Thompson as a teen
(Photograph printed with permission from Jerry Uhl)

The chapters that follow are about Grandma, her children, the family's manufacturing business and how they relate to my daughter's title of "Miss Moonshine".

Chapter 3

A Little History

According to Webster, moonshine is defined as "illegally distilled whiskey, to distill liquor illegally, to operate an illegal still" and bootlegging is defined as "a: to carry (alcoholic liquor) on one's person illegally b: to manufacture, sell or transport for sale (alcoholic liquor) contrary to law."

The *Encyclopedia of Appalachia* and *Moonshiners and Prohibitionists* further explain moonshiners in our country, especially those in the Appalachian culture, as being of European descent, most often Irish, self-sufficient and productive.

The Native Americans taught the European settlers how to grow corn. The early European settlers bartered with them often using whisky as an exchange for furs, corn, and other desirable services and items. Having used grains such as barley and rye to make whisky in their old countries, the colonists soon learned to distill corn into whisky too. It took far less space to store liquid grains than the dried ones and there was less chance of spoilage or other damages via varmints, fire, mold, mildew, etc. Whisky became an important part of early American industry, trade, and medical treatment, in addition to improving one's spirits. Since the people in the mountains were somewhat secluded, they didn't always get to schools to learn to read, or to have access to newspapers to keep them up to date on new laws, taxes, etc. Therefore, they did not register their stills, or pay taxes on their homemade products.

Wikipedia, "Ohio History Central", the previously named references, and other history books tell us there was a Whisky Rebellion in this great country in 1791. Congress passed a tax on liquor. Smaller manufacturers had to pay more taxes per gallon than the big businesses that produced larger quantities. The tax was to be paid in cash, and at that time few people had the cash to pay it. Local people gave the excise collectors a tough time and did not want excise houses in their communities. Therefore, they rebelled with some violence. By November of 1794, General George Washington was called into western Pennsylvania with the militia to put a stop to it and to aid in collection of the tax.

All who were held prisoner for the rebellion were exonerated. No doubt General Washington had something to do with that. The *Encyclopedia of Appalachia* states on page 478,

> "In 1799, after retiring from the nation's first presidency, George Washington is reported to have had a rye distillery that produced 11,000 gallons of whiskey at a then-handsome profit of $7,500.00."

Much of today's literature describes Appalachian people as religious. Some even call us Bible beaters. We were taught at an early age about the first miracle of Jesus, turning the water into wine at a wedding celebration in Cana. (John 2:11) Jesus didn't make lemonade, Kool-Aid, decaf coffee, iced tea, or any cola or soda. He made wine for folks to celebrate and be happy. So why in the world would there ever be a national movement against drinking alcoholic beverages led by people who claimed to be good Christians who were looking out for poor sinners who drank liquor?

Since ancient times the use of alcoholic beverages for medicinal purposes has been widespread in medical treatments of various kinds. The rise in scientific medicine after the Civil War led the way for the changing views of medical practitioners.

By 1916, there were many folks on the "no alcohol" bandwagon. An online temperance and prohibition article from Ohio State University states a resolution passed in June of 1917, at the annual meeting of the American Medical Association. It read as follows:

> "Whereas, We believe that the use of alcohol is detrimental to the human economy and Whereas, its use in therapeutics as a tonic or stimulant or for food has no scientific value; therefore Be it Resolved, That the American Medical Association is opposed to the use of alcohol as a beverage; and Be it Further Resolved, That the use of alcohol as a therapeutic agent should be further discouraged. "

The same article states, "Nevertheless, the prohibition laws allowed medicinal use of alcoholic beverages through prescription." (The prohibition laws also allowed the distribution of wine for sacramental purposes.)

Evidently there were places clergy and pharmacies could legally obtain liquor to fulfill medically-prescribed or sacrament-sanctioned alcoholic beverages, whether or not the American Medical Association was against it.

Ted Schwarz, in his biography of Joseph P. Kennedy, on page 95, wrote about Joe being a bootlegger and connected him with Al Capone, and alcohol for medicinal and sacramental purposes, on page 96:

> "There was also legal alcohol during Prohibition and Joe may have been a part of that world as well."

Schwarz continued in the same paragraph of page 96 by stating:

> "Doctors often prescribed alcohol in one form or another, and pharmacists could legally both stock and sell what would be illegal elsewhere. Naturally many men and women attempted to convince their physicians that they were afflicted with whatever liquor might "cure", and many doctors could be bribed to prescribe liquor "just in case" it would help."

David Koskoff, another Joseph P. Kennedy biographer, further verifies Joe Kennedy's participation in alcohol for medicinal purposes. Koskoff wrote, on pages 51 and 52, about how Joe used his British Ambassadorship and Roosevelt's son, Jimmie, to influence Winston Churchill and make a deal with his Somerset Importers business and the Haig & Haig British Distillers. Then Koskoff continues on page 53 with:

> "Back home, Kennedy received 'medical' permits to bring in two huge shipments of Scotch prior to repeal."

Around World War I, The Anti-Saloon League succeeded in getting the Eighteenth Amendment ratified into the United States Constitution, effective January 16, 1919, "outlawing the sale and manufacture of alcohol in the entire country". Well, as you know, that didn't last long.

On December 5, 1933, the Twenty-first Amendment to the United States Constitution repealed the Eighteenth Amendment.

Even though alcoholic beverages were legal if manufacturers were registered and paid taxes, there were still many people far removed from legal distilleries who made liquor for their own use, or for bartering. The early American people were self-sufficient. They grew and ate their own crops, raised and smoked their own tobacco, butchered the livestock they owned or hunted wild game for food. Making their own clothes, preserving their own food, and making their candles, soap, homebrew, wine and whisky were all part of their self-sufficiency. Folks felt the government was digging a little too deep into their pockets, especially as the Great Depression hit. Not only did the government control tax collection, it started limiting purchases. Even if a person had money to buy what he or she wanted, through rationing stamps, people were limited or rationed in what they could buy.

Blue Ration Stamps from WW II

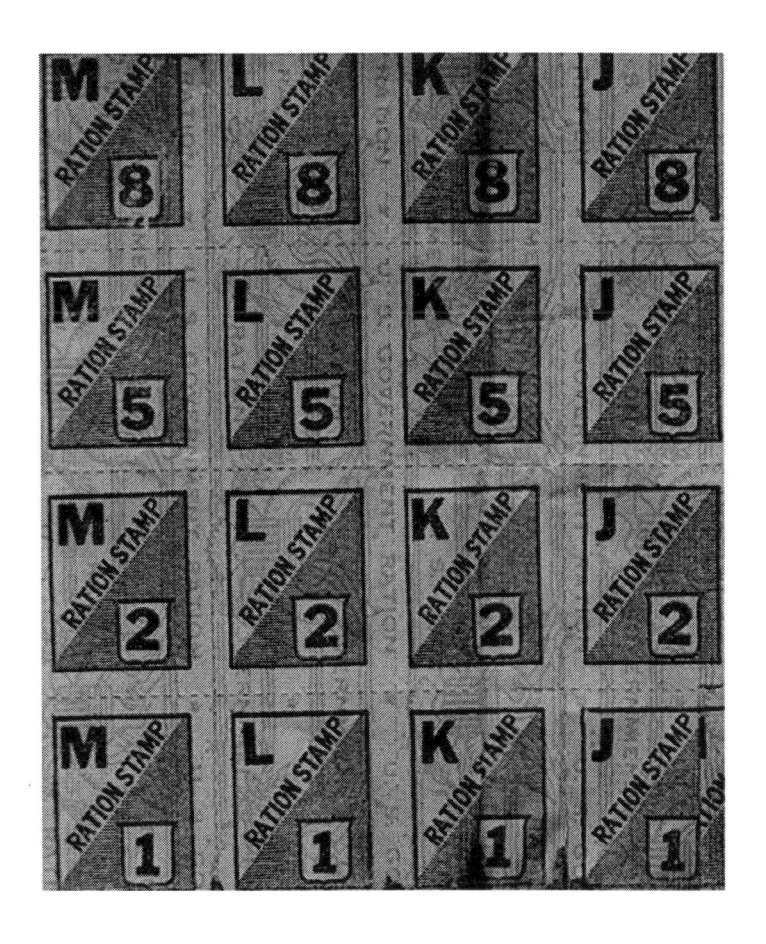

Red Ration Stamps from WWII

Revenuers (or tax enforcers) from the Internal Revenue Service, were frequently considered the "bad guys". They interfered with the common way of life.

Al Capone (01/17/1899 to 01/25/1947), a noted gangster in American history, got away with murder and numerous other syndicated crimes, but God forbid it in Uncle Sam's land, he'd ever get away with owing funds to the United States Internal Revenue Service. Of all the crimes he supposedly committed, income tax evasion is the charge that got him caught, tried, convicted and sentenced to prison.

The Appalachian community did not look upon bootleggers as criminals, but as folks trying to make a living during hard times, putting bread on the table to feed their families, creating manufacturing jobs in a poor economy, and providing goods and services to folks who wanted their product.

Local sheriffs, constables, police officers, and other officials didn't interfere much with the sale and distribution of moonshine. They probably enjoyed drinking it as much as the next fellow. No doubt, some of them or their kin were actually involved in some way. Far be it from me to question the integrity of any lawmen, as most are honest, dedicated employees. My great-uncle, Ray Thornton, was one of them. However, most folks did not consider revenuers with the esteem they revered the locally elected officers.

In an old, undated newspaper article from the *Ironton Tribune* entitled "Enormous Still", Special Dry Officers Willard Mays, Forest Dalton and George Neal found a still between Goldcamp's Station and Superior. Since the men were titled "Special Dry Officers", one could presume the date was during the Prohibition Era (1919-1933). The still, with a "thumping" compartment, was measured by court stenographer Earl Griffith to have held 165 gallons of moonshine and was described as having the appearance of having been in operation for several years. The article further stated, "The men who were operating it must have seen the approach of officers in plenty of time to make a safe get away [sic]."

Shown above are: Willard Mays, Forest Dalton and George Neal (stooped to right of still) beside the Lawrence County Courthouse with an "enormous still" they recovered during Prohibition. The photo was provided by Gail Webb and is printed with permission from Michael Caldwell, editor of *The Ironton Tribune.*

Other Tribune articles from February through October of 1939 mention:

> "Fred Griffith and Charles Shope of Upper Township arrested by federal agents Sunday on a charge of operating an illegal still and both were removed to Portsmouth prison to await arraignment before U.S. Commissioner, F.R. Ross. A boiler still, mash and equipment was confiscated in connection with the arrest, agents charge." *(Ironton Tribune* February 27, 1939)

> "John Riffitt and Turkey Peters arrested Sunday by State Agent West and City Patrolmen Wileman and Haas on charges of possessing untaxed whiskey, were to be given a hearing this afternoon before Police Justice George C. Hugger. Officers, who arrested the two men on the north side, charge Riffitt had a gallon of liquor in his possession and Peters had three gallons."

> "Henry Mason, colored, charged with possessing untaxed liquor, was fined $50 and cost [sic] in the court of Police Judge George Hugger today."

An article from *The Ironton Tribune* dated October 29, 1939, is headlined as follows:

"Scioto And Lawrence Liquor Ring Defrauded Government Of $20,000 In Tax Evasion

Seventeen Defendants Admit Guilt As Inquiry Into Conspiracy Is Launched"

The article, a bit confusing as written states,

"Cincinnati, Oh. Oct. 28-Twenty-eight of the 35 defendants charged with complicity with liquor conspiracy "rings" in Scioto and Lawrence Counties, Ohio, in the last three years, appeared before Judge Draffel yesterday to plead to the charges. Of the Cincinnati defendants eight pleaded guilty, and all of the others, not guilty. Trials are set for November 3 and 6. Of those pleading to the Scioto and Lawrence county indictments 17 admitted guilt. Trial of the others was set for court Wednesday, November 1.

The Cincinnatians who pleaded guilty were Garland Pearson, 912 Betts Street; Charles Cotton, 1872 John Street; Bernice Coleman, 816 Mound Street; Willis Robinson, 117 West Fourth Street; Jessie Maghni, 922 Harriet Street; William Lloyd, no address; Ben Russell, 814 West Eighth Street; and Stella Jones, 1038 Oedler Street.

Three pleading guilty in the two other indictments were Paul Yates, Delaware,

Ohio; Marion Yates, and Thomas Delong Pedro, Ohio; Bill Jones, New Boston; Allen Jones, Portsmouth; Blaine Gullett, Robert Adams and Virgil Adams, New Boston; Robert Crisp, Charles Roof, John Mason, and Wilson Liggins, Portsmouth; Morris Hamilton, Jesse Pendleton, Abberman Stone, and John H. Hayes, New Boston. Federal alcohol tax unit agents said the two rings [sic] operation in Cincinnati have defrauded the government of $50,000 in revenue taxes on liquor distributed illicitly; that in Scioto and Lawrence Counties liquor which should have netted the government approximately $20,000 was 'moonshined' and illegally distributed."

Now, let's concentrate on that $20,000 in tax revenue from the smaller ring in Scioto and Lawrence Counties. According to information found on the web at http://www.thesunsfinancialdiary.com/plll/federal-minimum-wage-725hour-chart-day/, the federal minimum wage for 1939 was only ($00.30) thirty cents per hour. So in an eight hour day a person would gross ($2.40) two dollars and forty cents, or ($12.00) twelve dollars per week. How much could a gallon of whisky have cost in 1939? That was well past the end of Prohibition.

An eighty-nine-year-old friend from Lawrence County advised me he had paid thirty cents a pint for moonshine in 1939. With eight pints in a gallon, that would be $2.40 per gallon. I can't find any charts or websites that give me the tax on liquor at that time. However, I did find on google.com through a whisky price history search that

> "On December 22, 1933, The United States Chamber of Commerce board of directors, the advisory council of the Federal Reserve Board and numerous others... In Pennsylvania, distilleries closed after the Legislature passed a bill taxing whisky $2 a gallon, the distillers contending they could not operate..."

If we take that $20,000 the government approximated in lost revenue for the ring in Lawrence and Scioto Counties and figure a tax of two dollars ($2.00) on a gallon of moonshine that sold for only ($2.40) then those men would have sold approximately 10,000 gallons of moonshine in three years.

If we figure the minimum wage was ($12.00) twelve dollars per week, then the annual salary of twelve dollars per week times fifty-two weeks would be an annual gross wage of six-hundred twenty-four dollars. (12 X 52 = 624). Ten thousand gallons of moonshine sold at two dollars and forty cents per gallon would be twenty-four thousand dollars gross ($24,000.00) in three years. (Divide the $24,000 by the three years mentioned in the previous news article, 24000 ÷ 3 = 8000 per year.)

You'd think these moonshiners would have been rich making eight thousand dollars ($8,000.00) per year when six-hundred twenty-four dollars ($624.00) was the gross minimum wage at the time, but I personally knew many moonshiners and they were not rich. I also know these men did not work in rings - families maybe, but not rings. It was each man (or family) for himself.

My guess is the revenuers drastically over estimated the lost tax revenues from unregistered stills. This further contributed to their being unpopular with the general public.

From the names of those listed previously in *The Ironton Tribune* articles in this chapter, in the next chapter we will focus on the two men mentioned from Lawrence County in the October 29, 1939, story. The two men are Marion Yates and Thomas Delong.

Chapter 4

The Family Manufacturing Business

My maternal uncle Marion Yates, mentioned in the *Ironton Tribune* article in Chapter 3 (on page 38) as part of a moonshining ring, was born October 21, 1910. He was the second child of Walter Neal Yates and Cora Alice Delawder Yates and resided with them on Elkins Creek. Uncle Marion attended school in Aid Township, Lawrence County, Ohio, where he met and later married Ida Waugh (early in the 1930's). He died of cancer October 31, 1955, at the age of forty-five. I remember him as a handsome gentleman. He was a kind person, loving father, devoted husband and good provider. He was honest, a hard worker, a patriotic American, and a World War II veteran. He had a friendly disposition and a pleasant sense of humor.

When he died I was almost eight. In all my life, I have never heard even one person say anything negative about him.

Pat Yates Leeper, Uncle Marion's only surviving daughter and oldest child, was born April 7, 1937. She can remember some of the moonshine era, especially how Uncle Earl would volunteer to fetch the cows and be gone for days. The cows wanted to be milked and came in for the evening milking on their own. Grandma worried about her missing son because of his heart condition and sent his brothers to search for him.

According to Pat, he was usually found near the still with an empty jug, sleeping off a hangover.

Earl Yates, Justice of the Peace

Pat also recalled how Grandma sewed pockets on her underskirts to hold her money and having seen a cow kick Grandma while she cleaned its teats for milking. Grandma, who rarely ever lost her temper, hit that cow with her milk bucket. Seeing Grandma lose her cool with the cow made quite an impression on Pat, who also has fond memories of her dad, Marion, having bought presents of black silk socks and tailor-made cigarettes for his afflicted baby brother, our Uncle Joe.

Uncle Marion's only other surviving child is Harold Lee Yates. Harold was born June 8, 1940, while his father was serving one year and one day of federal time in the U.S. Reformatory located in Chillicothe, Ohio. Harold told me about his dad relating stories from the moonshine era regarding selling his homemade whisky to the students at Marshall University in Huntington, West Virginia. Uncle Marion was amazed at how the college kids always had money for moonshine, especially since it cost so much for tuition, room, board and books. Harold also told me that he remembers going with his dad up a hollow behind a grocery store at the corner of Hog Run Road and State Route 141 during the early 1950's to buy and sell moonshine. We'll discuss that a little more in detail later in the next chapter.

Thomas Delong's name was also mentioned in the newspaper article, along with Uncle Marion's, as being a part of a moonshine ring in Lawrence County. Tom and his siblings lived near the Yates family on what we called Rucker Ridge. The Delong family was distant kin to the Yates family, but the precise relationship via my Great-great-great grandmother, Ann Delong Yates, wife of Benjamin Yates, has not been determined.

The Paul Yates from Delaware, Ohio, mentioned in the article is not the nephew of Marion (Paul David Yates, son of Forrest, who was a small child in 1939). Although I have sought information about this particular Paul Yates and his connection to Uncle Marion, I haven't come up with much to date.

Joe and Babe (Uriah) Rucker, brothers, also lived on Rucker Ridge and they were Grandma's first cousins. Their mother was the sister of Joseph Delawder, Grandma's father. Therefore, Joe and Babe were my third cousins.

Marion Yates in WW II uniform, 1943

I have unsuccessfully tried to contact the children of Thomas Delong and Raymond Delong. However, cousins, nephews and neighbors have volunteered information and acknowledged the two brothers' involvement in the manufacture of moonshine.

It is known that Tom continued manufacturing spirits throughout his life, even after his arrest. Reportedly, one still was under his house and another was covered by a pile of brush on Homeless Road at Kitts Hill, across the road from the Alvin Harper home. Although there has been some indication by others that Tom and Raymond's brother, Robert, was involved, it has not been substantiated by public record or by the family.

There is proof the Yates/Delawder family was involved in their manufacturing business as early as 1923. An article from *The Portsmouth Daily Times,* dated October 25, 1923, stated:

"Taken to U.S. Court

Ironton, O., Oct. 25- On an indictment returned by a federal grand jury, Evans and Rufus Barnett and Albert Delawder were arrested by Sheriff Dement and Deputy Mat Wilson. A United States marshal came to this city and took the men to Cincinnati for arraignment.

The men were recently arrested at Cannon's Creek where it is alleged they were operating two stills. Three other men were taken at the same time and place.

At Prosecutor Elkins' office it was announced that those convicted of liquor offenses have in many cases employed every tactic and technicality possible to secure delay in execution of sentences pronounced by appeal and otherwise, that it was not deemed advisable to eliminate these in part, by taking such cases to the federal court."

The above photo is of some of the Delawder brothers in the in the early 1900's. Row 1: Hobart, Amos and Ernest. Row 2: John and Albert

Albert Delawder was my grandmother's (Cora Alice Delawder Yates) brother. He was born September 23, 1887, to Joseph Perry Delawder and Lydia Ann Neal Delawder in

Aid, Ohio. In 1919 he married Fairnetta Susan Leffingwell (Aunt Nettie). They parented three children: William (Bill), Dorothy and (Roy) Kenneth. According to a Portsmouth newspaper, Great-uncle Albert was arrested for operating two stills in 1923. According to another newspaper article in *The Ironton Tribune* in 1926, Albert was killed in an auto accident in Minnesota on his way home from working in the harvest fields.

Arrested in 1923 with Great-uncle Albert were two brothers who lived near the Delawder family, Rufus G. Barnett and Evans Barnett, sons of William B. Barnett and Ellen Tiller Barnett. Rufus was born about 1904 in Virginia and was listed in the 1920 U.S. Census as living in Aid, Ohio, as a sixteen-year-old. He married Nellie Mart and lived his whole life in Lawrence County. A *Newark Advocate* newspaper article stated:

> "Squirrel Hunter Really Not Lost;
> Holed Up In Cave
> IRONTON, Ohio (AP)
>
> Fifty volunteers led by sheriff's deputies beat the backcountry bush all night Thursday looking for a lost squirrel hunter. They didn't find him.
> Rufus Barnett, 52, the hunter, walked into his home, Rt. 2, Pedro, in time for breakfast. He explained he got lost and spent the night in a cave only about two miles from his house."

Rufus died at Pedro, Lawrence County, Ohio, in 1981. His older brother, who went by the names of Evans Robert Barnett and Robert Evans Barnett (from 1910 census records) was the oldest child of William Barnett. Evans was also born in Virginia.

"Evan" Barnett is mentioned in *The Times Recorder* of Zanesville in an article dated October 6, 1933. It stated as follows:

> "Acquitted on One Charge Arrested
> on Another
> GALLIPOLIS, O (AP)
>
> Acquitted by a jury of a charge of burglarizing the home of Fred Carter, a Gallia county farmer, Evan Barnett was immediately re-arrested in the county court room here today to answer charges of robbing Carter's granary. Two alleged companions have pleaded guilty.
>
> Barnett was formerly a constable in Lawrence County."

Ancestry.com verified a Robert Evans Barnett from Pedro, Ohio, was born in 1901 and married a Bessie Blanche Loper. He died June 15, 1937.

According to newspaper articles and acquaintances of the Barnett brothers, Evans Barnett was murdered via multiple gunshots, along with a Mae Davis (Lewis), a noted resident of Third and Buckhorn Streets in Ironton, on New Castle Ridge near Ellisonville.

A June 1937 *Ironton Tribune* article stated:

> "The crime created considerable excitement in Ironton due to the fact

both victims are rather well known. Mrs. Lewis has been a resident of the North Third Street neighborhood for many years and has been arrested a number of times on liquor and other charges. Barnett gained notoriety during prohibition years when he served as a federal agent and later as a crusading officer of the Squire Boggs court. He was paroled only seven months ago after serving a penitentiary sentence for robbery in Gallia County."

News stories stated Evans and Mae were involved with the mob out of Chicago, were murdered in Cleveland, and their bodies dumped on New Castle Ridge. Although I could not locate *The Ironton Tribune* article that gave all the details and told who murdered them, as it was close to a year after the incident occurred, two elderly gentlemen who knew the Barnetts and are reliable sources have both told me Mae and Evans were murdered by the Dingledines from Mad River, near Springfield, Ohio.

Another *Ironton Tribune* article, "Merry-Making At Murder Scene", "Short Time Before Series of Shots Heard", indicated the victims were acquainted with their murderers and thought they were going off to a party when in fact they were taken off to be slain.

One of my elderly cousins, ninety-year-old Wayne Rucker, told me he was actually present when the sheets were removed from the bodies (of Mae and Evans) on the mortician's slab. They were both naked and shot full of bullet holes from a Tommy gun. At the time of his observation the corpses were at Golden's Funeral Home being prepared for burial.

There are many articles on ancestry.com from newspapers across Ohio (Springfield, Marion, Lima, Elyria, Newark, Hamilton, etc.) about Henry and Harry Dingledine, a father (Harry) and son criminal team, during the 1930s. In addition to murdering Mae and Evans, they escaped jail, had a shoot-out with law enforcement officers from several states and killed three peace officers. There are articles available (example: Henry was once arrested in Marion in a stolen auto and turned over to authorities in Bellefontaine for a robbery charge) about them and another partner in crime, Harry Chapman (a mobster from Chicago), and their robberies, thefts and multiple murders in many states, including Wisconsin, Michigan, Texas, Utah, Pennsylvania, Indiana and Iowa, also on ancestry.com. There are photographs of them on the internet from the Ohio Penitentiary and from a Springfield newspaper. I did not seek permission to print them because the men were neither Appalachian moonshiners, nor officers of the law.

Harley Vanmeter, an eighty-nine-year-old Pedro resident and family friend, told me he read about Chapman, the Dingledines, Mae Davis Lewis and their gang, the Wolves of Mad River, in *The True Detectives Magazine* when he was a boy. He also remembered the photo of Mae in a polka dot dress included with the article. There were more articles that suggested Evans was also a part of their gang, which was affiliated with the mob in Chicago and Cleveland, but I have not had any success in finding copies of the old magazine online or through the library.

Killing the law officers was their dooming crime. The Dingledines were executed in "old sparky" on April 13, 1939, at the old Ohio Penitentiary in Columbus, Ohio. It was the only verifiable father and son electric chair execution ever in Ohio. Their Franklin County death certificates (24062 and 24063) are listed online.

It would not surprise me if information turned up linking them to the death of Great-uncle Albert. Fortunately, he did not die with them. However, there were also some tales about his fatal accident of 1926, but the newspaper article in the *Ironton Tribune* about the tragedy was quite vague and second-handed. It read as follows:

"WAS KILLED IN AUTO ACCIDENT

Ironton Man Returning Home When Hit By Car

> Funeral services for Albert Delawder, who was killed in an automobile accident in Minnesota, will be held at the Aaron's [sic] Creek U. B. Church Sunday afternoon at 2 o'clock with Rev. Kempner in charge. Internment will be in Aaron's [sic] Creek cemetery under the direction of Mortician Phillips, of Waterloo.
>
> Particulars of Mr. Delawder's death were received here today. He has been working in the harvest fields and with two men from Illinois was driving from Fargo, N. D., to the Twin Cities last Friday evening. They ran out of gas and Mr. Delawder with one of his companions started walking to the nearest village for a can of gasoline. Mr. Delawder was struck by an automobile driven by Ray McDowell, of Hancock, Minn. He was picked up unconscious with both legs and one arm broken and internal injuries, and died in a hospital at 4 o'clock Saturday morning.

A coroner's inquest exonerated the driver who struck him from any blame, rendering a verdict of accidental death.

Mr. Delawder is survived by his widow, three brothers, Ernest and Homer, of Elkins Creek, Amos, of Masquon, Ill, who arrived here Friday for the funeral and one sister, Mrs. Neil [sic] Yates, of Pedro."

There are many mistakes within the preceding article. Albert's three children were not mentioned. He had three brothers in Illinois and three in Lawrence County, Ohio, in addition to his sister, Mrs. Cora (Walter Neal) Yates. The names of his companions were not mentioned. Some have suspected his death to have been related to his affiliation with the moonshine business. No one knows for sure if the mob was involved, but who would risk his life to find out what went on that far away, especially when one is already dead and the law could be bought. It was only wise to grieve in silence.

One would also wonder why he would go to North Dakota or to Minnesota to work in the harvest fields when Ohio, Indiana and Illinois are the greatest farm states in the Union and all are much closer to home for a family man. Besides, he had brothers living in Illinois, should he want to work in harvest fields outside of Ohio. Also one might question how a coroner could determine if an automobile hit a person intentionally or by accident, unless his inquest might have something to do with the influence of the Chicago mob.

Evans Barnett is the only person in this book involved in moonshining with any verification (preceding newspaper articles) of involvement in any other crime.

It has not been determined who the three other men mentioned arrested in *The Portsmouth Times* article with Albert Delawder and the Barnett brothers were, but they were probably neighbors and/or relatives.

A third cousin, Lenora Miller, recently told me the original home of Joseph and Lydia Delawder, our great-grandparents (parents of Cora, Amos, Albert, Hobart, Ernest, John, Homer, and Everett), was on Aarons Creek, near Cannons Creek. When Joseph Delawder died, Lydia and her sons moved to Elkins Creek, near where her daughter, Cora Yates, already lived. Lenora is the granddaughter of Homer Delawder, Grandma's brother, through her mother, Helen Delawder Miller. Homer and his family also lived on Elkins Creek.

All of my life, I have heard about Mom's family being moonshiners, but not until researching information on my *Appalachian Childhood* last year, did I realize the scope of the involvement and that Grandma was also arrested along with her sons and brothers. This general information was provided to me by a third cousin, Kathy Delawder Akers (granddaughter of Homer Delawder via her father Clarence Delawder). Kathy visited our home often as a child, but now lives in Kentucky. Last year she read an old, undated newspaper article to me over the telephone. The article stated my grandmother was arrested for moonshining and was the first clue that indicated my grandma was involved. Once over the initial shock from Kathy's piece of printed verification, it all began to sink in. With my memory of Uncle Forrest's stories and other bits of information obtained from Kathy and my cousin, Norman Humphrey, I started making phone calls and visits and writing letters to various people and offices, including: the Ironton Tribune, the Lawrence County Clerk of Courts, the Lawrence

County Sheriff's Department, the Lawrence County Public Library, the Delaware County Historical Society, the Federal Bureau of Prisons in Washington, D.C., the Ohio Federal District Courts in Columbus and Cincinnati, the National Archives in Chicago, the Lawrence County Recorder's Office, the Lawrence County Historical Society, the Delaware County Genealogical Society and Phillips Funeral Home. I also researched information on ancestry.com, and some other online resources. Everyone contacted was helpful and most had valuable information to contribute.

Norman remembered stories our grandfather, Walter Neal Yates, told him about his brother, Charles Yates, making moonshine on the home place of our great-grandfather, Isaac Yates, Senior, on Aarons Creek, the same property now owned by the George McClure family. (The house and land went from Great-grandfather Isaac to his oldest son, Charles, a lifelong bachelor born in 1876.) It seems the revenuers suspected Great-uncle Charley of having a still and went to his farm to investigate. The still was naturally well hidden in a gully approximately twenty feet deep and covered with so many trees, undergrowth and brush that the gully wasn't even visible, let alone the still. The government employees searched his house, outbuildings and the large farm from one end to the other, but found nothing. Uncle Charley had figured the internal revenue workers would eventually be around, so he cleverly prepared an unexpected hiding place for the spirits he sold. His whisky was hidden inside the pant legs of some bib overalls he kept hanging on a clothesline. The revenuers left discouraged because they found nothing. Although suspected, Charley Yates was never caught.

Charles Yates during WW I

Thus, my great-uncles on both Grandma's and Grandpa's sides of the family were in the business of distilling illegal whisky before their sons got into it.

It has been awesome to discover all of the available data and how it ties into our culture and my family's, Lawrence County's, Ohio's, and our nation's history.

From the one newspaper article mentioning Uncle Marion in the preceding chapter, the information that follows was obtained. There is absolutely no doubt (since other articles regarding the family were found as verification) that for generations my family was actively engaged in the business of manufacturing moonshine for profit.

Chapter 5

Business Partners

Accepting any information that my sweet maternal grandmother would have ever done anything illegal was difficult. I did not want to believe it. I can remember participating in family card games and hearing stories from my Uncle Forrest about his moonshine days and how he and his brothers did time, but in all my life, until talking with Cousin Kathy, I had not heard anyone mention Grandma's involvement. Kathy also told me she had heard her grandfather, Grandma's brother, Homer Clarence Delawder, was somehow involved.

I started seeking knowledge by asking the few people still alive who would remember. I figured if I could get enough information to write some letters, I'd find the truth about my grandmother.

There was a rumor that Uncle Earl took Grandma's rap so she wouldn't have to go to prison, but it has been proven, Uncle Earl was truly involved.

There is interesting family and local folklore about various incidents, such as Uncle Homer's and Uncle Albert's deaths, Grandma's arrest, Agent Coach and other related characters. Most of it is verifiable. However, I have learned, depending on who tells the story, the data became adapted to prevent hurt or embarrassment to the widows and offspring. Thus, I will pass over some of the more entertaining lore and try to stick with the facts.

Walter Neal Yates and Cora Delawder Yates produced eight children. One of their children, Shirley, died during infancy. Earl was the oldest child, then Marion, Edna, Forrest, Isaac, Joseph and Vedna.

Cousin Norman advised me he'd been told that since Uncle Earl wasn't much into work, he became the lookout and blew a conch shell as a horn to warn the others when revenuers approached. (This piece of information was confirmed once the court report was received.) Hobart Delawder, one of Grandma's bachelor brothers, was caught, handcuffed to a sapling, and cried real tears, while revenuers chased the rest of the family. There is no evidence to substantiate anyone else being caught at that particular time, but there is verification regarding Uncle Hobart's arrest.

Because Uncle Ike (Isaac, Mom's brother, not Grandpa's brother Isaac or father Isaac), according to several family members, was under the age of twenty-one at the time of his arrest, he did not go to federal court, but was taken to the Lawrence County Courthouse, where Norman saw him in handcuffs. Uncle Ike was waiting for his hearing and for Agent Coach, the arresting revenuer, to appear.

Uncle Ike was described as an angry young man, who frustratingly stated he wanted to throw Coach over the railing and down the stairs to meet his doom. Court records can't be accessed because they are stored in the courthouse attic and are probably covered in pigeon dung.

Some of Uncle Ike's family members and Norman have related to me that he was given the option to go into the service during World War II in lieu of a prison sentence. Some of the family members also advised that he had told stories about driving the moonshine delivery vehicle from the age of twelve and earning the money from this job to buy his first automobile.

Considering Isaac started deliveries at age 12, and he was born January 25, 1918, the family had to have been

Floyd Matney, Lonnie Conway and Isaac Yates at age 14 on viewer's right (Photo dated by car license plate as 1932)

manufacturing prior to 1930, during the Prohibition Era, and probably long before, since Great-uncle Albert was arrested in 1923.

Aunt Martha, Uncle Ike's widow, shared a story with me about Uncle Ike having made a solo delivery of a car loaded with moonshine when he was only twelve to Van Leer, Kentucky. The drive, as per mapquest.com computation, was approximately ninety-five miles one way from the Yates home. Roads weren't as good then and vehicles didn't travel as fast. Although Ike was very tall for his age, it was a long, dangerous trip for a boy to be on alone, yet a twelve-year-old child wouldn't be suspected of making a moonshine run at all, and certainly not one of that magnitude, with no adults to protect him. Revenuers weren't apt to arrest a twelve-year-old child traveling alone on federal charges either, which is probably the very reason young Isaac drove the vehicle alone.

I can't believe Grandma knew anything about such a trip, or she would never have let him travel alone at such a young age.

Loretta Lynn and her sister, Crystal Gayle, are from Butcher Holler at Van Leer. In 1979, when my daughters were small, we drove Aunt Martha there from Lawrence County to visit and reminisce. Even though the highways were greatly improved, it was a long trip and Butcher Holler was still primitive with outhouses in use. It was a remnant of an old mining town and had a rugged general store that was run by Loretta's and Crystal's family. The folks were friendly and invited us into their home, store and to use their outdoor toilet. It's no wonder Uncle Ike felt safe driving there as a child.

Sometime during his teens, Uncle Ike was in the Civilian Conservation Corps, therefore he did not work continuously in the family manufacturing business.

Norman remembers reading an Ironton newspaper article about a "Juvenile Caught Red-handed" in a moonshine raid while visiting his paternal grandmother at Willow Wood, Ohio. The article stated the juvenile was sitting under the still with a jug resting between his legs to catch the whisky as it dripped from the distillery hose. Even as a child, Norman knew the article was about his and my Uncle Ike.

Given the choice of jail or war by a Lawrence County judge, young Isaac Yates chose war, joined the Army, and spent much of his next six years in Europe where he fought in numerous battles, including the famous Battle of the Bulge. During his time in the military, he won many medals and awards. While home on a furlough in March of 1946, he married Martha Kimble.

Isaac Yates in WW II uniform

A wedding photo of Isaac Orlyn Yates
and Martha Kimble Yates

    Before I was six, Uncle Ike obtained a job in a steel mill and moved his family to Lorain County. Aunt Martha and their four daughters, Cora Sonja, Sharon Dee, Yvonne Carol, and Tammy Shellene, still remain in that area. Once honorably discharged from the Army, Uncle Ike never made any more moonshine. He died in 1993.

Uncle Forrest was born in October of 1915. He married Garnett Evicks as a teen and fathered their only son at the young age of twenty. They divorced and Garnett married one of the neighboring Waugh brothers, Ernest. Uncle Forrest joined the Army during World War II and left Paul David, his only son at the time, in Grandma's care. He never married again until 1947. His second wife was Hazel Lewis. They had three children: Walter Richard, Forrest Ray and Dianna Kay. Aunt Hazel and all of her children currently reside in Marion, Ohio.

Forrest Rose Yates during WW II

Forrest Yates was my favorite uncle. Dad had no brothers and he knew Mom's brothers before the war. Uncle Forrest and Dad actually were stationed in California together during their time in the military. They remained lifelong friends and admired one another. Dad often complimented Uncle Forrest's ability to find or create gainful employment. He was a wonderful provider for his family, a master distiller, a fine woodworker, gardener, father, husband and uncle. I spent many nights as a child in his home and at Grandma's house playing with his children, which was always a joy. As an adult, Uncle Forrest continued to visit my home often. He was truly a jolly old fellow and enjoyed playing cards, smoking cigars, telling jokes and having a shot or two with family and friends. My daughters also loved him, enjoyed playing family card games with him and were entertained by listening to his stories of the days of moonshine, travels and merriment. He died in Marion General Hospital in 1998. Malissa was a student nurse there at the time and losing him was devastating to her as a nurse and as a great-niece. We all miss him and have fond memories of his great sense of humor.

I don't know what year Uncle Forrest started in the manufacturing business, but knew he had the reputation of being the master of the trade. Family members and friends have told me he continued to distill in Marion County into the late 1970's and often delivered his wares to folks in Lawrence County. The copper still he used at that time and made from an old copper washing machine currently exists, but not in the family. The master aged his whisky in wooden barrels charred inside with charcoal to give the

The above photo is from left to right: an unknown, Forrest Yates and William L. Thornton, my dad, in San Francisco, California, during World War II.

finished product a golden color. He blended his spirits to no more than 100 proof alcohol and spoke of looking for "frogs' eyes", or bubbles, in the solution to determine its proof. In the 1930's, he was stopped numerous times by the revenuers, but was not easy to catch with evidence against him. He regularly drove Grandma to town to sell her eggs at Hannan's Grocery Store and frequently was stopped along the way by authorities to check the vehicle for moonshine-related items.

The Yates brothers pleasantly recalled their manufacturing days and told how they tied down the springs on their automobiles so revenuers could not tell by looking when the vehicle had a full load or was empty.

Hobart Delawder, Grandma's brother, was my favorite great-uncle. He spent a great deal of time at our house and at Grandma's. I never remember him ever having talked about moonshining. He was very particular of his conversation around children and young ladies. However, I have seen him inebriated on numerous occasions. When we moved to Ironton from Kitts Hill, he regularly came to our house after the bars closed and yelled for my sisters and me to come open the gate to the picket fence for him. Under the influence and in the dark of night, even with the streetlights, he couldn't seem to be able to find the sidewalk or the latch on the gate. We ran out in a hurry to open it for him so our neighbors wouldn't complain about his yelling. There are not enough good things I could say about this dear man. He assisted Grandma in raising her children. He was a World War I veteran. He retired from a steel mill further north. He never missed assisting with buying school clothes for my siblings and me. He was constantly buying presents for Mom and all of her children. He bought every niece and great-niece (approximately 30 gals) a wristwatch upon completing the eighth grade, if the particular niece made a promise to him to complete high school. He helped pay for my senior trip to the New York World's Fair and bought me some new clothes to take on it. When we were smaller, he babysat my siblings and me so Mom and Dad could go out. The first one of us to get up in the morning received a silver dollar, usually me, and he smiled and said, "The early bird gets the worm." He had the reputation of being the finest corn picker, shucker and

My dear great-uncle
Hobart Delawder in 1963

shocker in the county. I can remember him making a cross from boards and attaching it with leather straps to his back to form a brace for support before going into the fields to work. He was a truly hardworking, honest man. Uncle Hobart loved the Cincinnati Reds and listened to all of their games on the radio, even when they were on TV. With all of his wonderful qualities, the dear man was at times a crying drunk. So, hearing the story of his crying like a baby when handcuffed by the revenuers to the sapling, was of no surprise to me. He also cried about missing his mother dear and sometimes, with a slight speech impediment, sang and recited poetry in her loving memory. He never married, was patriotic, kind, respectful of others, giving, encouraging and I loved him dearly. He died in 1971, when I was pregnant with my first child.

Once retired, Great-uncle Hobart often lived with his bachelor brother, Great-uncle Ernest Delawder. Uncle Ernie was in contrast to Uncle Hobart: he never bought any presents, rarely helped Grandma, was full of himself. Uncle Ernie was also a World War I veteran and retired from working in the steel mill. He managed to be intoxicated more than his siblings and was often requested to leave our home because Dad felt he had difficulty behaving properly in the presence of women and children. He liked to argue, was tidy and neat in appearance, and of short stature. He and Uncle Hobart often quarreled, as Uncle Ernie fussed with everyone when he was nursing a booze bottle, but Grandma tolerated him well. It was not unusual to hear folks compare Uncle Ernie to a little Bantam rooster.

Great-uncle Homer Clarence Delawder was born in 1899. He married Lona Nelson and they had two children, (Homer) Clarence and Helen. An article about his death appeared in an Ironton newspaper on August 3, 1931, and stated:

"Homer Delawder Killed In
Automobile Wreck Saturday

Injuries received in an automobile accident shortly before six o'clock Saturday evening, resulted fatally for Homer Delawder, 34 [sic], of Elkins Creek Road, in Aid Township.

Delawder died at the Marting Hospital at six o'clock from a crushed chest suffered when a car he was driving, accompanied by Ambrose Moore, 47, a neighbor, left the road about 200 yards from the Ike Yates home on the Elkins Creek highway.

Moore escaped with a slight laceration on the right side of the face and bruises about the body.

Delawder is said to have failed to make a right-hand turn, and the machine, a Ford Roadster, left the road, turning over three times. The top and glass in the sport roadster were crushed and both occupants were pinned inside the machine.

Wayne Kelly, 22, and Earl Yates, 24, brought Delawder to the hospital, where he died within a few minutes.

Ernest Delawder, only brother of the victim in this county, was arrested by Sheriff Bennett after a disturbance at the hospital. Delawder accused Kelly and Yates of killing his brother.

He was discharged from custody a short time later, however.

He said that he had heard Saturday morning that they were going to get his brother and that he didn't want him to leave home.

Delawder is survived by his widow, Lona, and two minor children, Clarence

and Helen; three brothers residing at
Maquon, Ill., Amos, John and Everett,
in addition to Ernest and one sister, Mrs.
Cora Yates, also survive.

Funeral services will be held Tuesday
afternoon at two o'clock at the home near
Oak Ridge Furnace. Rev. Kemper, of Franklin
Furnace, will officiate at the rites, and intern-
ment will be in the Nelson cemetery under
the direction of Undertaker Phillips of
Waterloo."

The article failed to mention two other brothers, Hobart and Albert Delawder.

One of Great-uncle Homer's granddaughters, Lenora Miller, advised me she was told her grandfather was on the way home from working at a cement plant when the accident occurred. She was also told there was fresh gravel in the road that had something to do with causing the tragedy, and that her grandfather succumbed instantly with a death grip on the steering wheel that needed to be pried loose in order to remove his body from the wreckage. What Lenora was told does not coincide with the information in the newspaper article.

Family rumor had it that Homer, who had been drinking, was on his way home from making moonshine deliveries when his fatality happened. However, there was nothing mentioned about it in the newspaper. Lenora related to me she had been told her grandfather refused to have anything to do with the family distillation business, except for making sugar purchases for his sister, Cora Delawder

Yates, my grandmother. Lenora also had been told her grandmother was at the scene of the accident, but that is not confirmed by the rest of the family or by the media either.

Although I was not born at the time, Uncle Ernie's behavior, as described in the newspaper article regarding Uncle Homer's death is not at all surprising to me. As I remember him, he was a cocky little guy who was often intoxicated and enjoyed starting arguments and picking fights. Because of his behaviors, he was not one of my favorite relatives.

The Isaac Yates property mentioned in the Homer Delawder article was that of my Great-uncle Ike, Grandpa's brother. His property bordered Grandma's. Wayne Kelly lived up the hollow beyond Grandma's house. Ambrose Moore lived near Uncle Homer's house. Ambrose's son, Edgar, lived across the road between Great-uncle Ike's and Great-uncle Homer's properties in a large green house. Earl Yates was a nephew to both Ernest and Homer Delawder. Had there actually been anything to Uncle Ernie's outburst and accusations, there would have been an investigation and talk within the family. One could only assume alcohol was involved in Uncle Ernie's behavior at the time of the arrest. He was probably released when he "sobered up".

When Edith and Edgar Moore moved from their green house around 1941, my grandfather Thornton and his family moved into it. Aunt Margaret, Aunt Marie and Aunt Mabel were all married at the time, so only Dad and Aunt Hanna were living with their parents in the green home. It was about that time my parents met. After their marriage, my brother Ronnie was born in that green house in 1942.

Ronnie told folks he was born feet first in a green house, leading them to believe it was a plant nursery. Mom didn't tell me he was exaggerating, but did point the house out to me as we drove by it on the way to Aunt Lona's to let me know it was an ordinary house with the exterior painted green.

It seems many of the fellows my uncles befriended were also in the distillation business. Their buddies who didn't distill were frequently customers or relatives. In making a connection with how Marion Yates ended up with a still in Delaware County near the border of Marion County, several folks come to mind.

Ambrose Moore was born at Rock Camp in Lawrence County in 1884 and died in the same county in 1960. However, at sometime he moved to and lived in Marion County, as his son, Edgar Moore, was born in Marion County in 1914. By association, Ambrose Moore was (verified by newspaper article) with Homer Delawder in the fatal accident, which some folks believe to have been moonshine delivery-related. Forrest Yates later lived in Marion County and died there. Family and friends have told me Ed Moore and Uncle Forrest remained close friends all of their lives. The Yates, Delawder and Moore families lived near the Waugh family who also moonshined. Some of the Waughs lived in Marion County in the 1930's, as did some of the family of Tom Jenkins, mentioned in a later chapter. Jonah Main is mentioned in an article from *The Marion Star,* another of the Yates /Delawder connections in Marion, Ohio, and was also associated with a Yates/Legg still in Delaware County, an adjoining county to Marion. The Main property was near the border of the two counties.

Like me not knowing of Grandma's involvement in the family business, there were/are others who didn't know about their particular relative either, as some things just were not discussed with women and children.

There were some stories passed through the generations that Homer Delawder had made a statement before his fatal accident about how fast he could take the curve at the foot of the hill, the very curve that took his life. Lenora is the only one who mentioned the new gravel having anything to do with the wreck. The old folks who remember still talk about that accident and Uncle Albert's accident in Minnesota. It is always sad when a young fellow dies and leaves a widow and small children behind.

There are also rumors that Albert Delawder's death was alcohol-related, but again, that would be difficult to prove at this time.

Family and friends have also told me Aunt Ida's father and brothers, the Waughs, were involved in manufacturing spirits, as were some of the Kelly family. I have been informed of moonshiners by the name of Pinkerman, Scott, Jenkins, Smith, Roberts, Barnett, Birchfield, Miller, Riffit, Shope, Griffith, Mason, Fradd, Sprouse, and more by newspaper articles, families and friends. Some never got caught. Some served time, others didn't. The involvement of some folks in moonshining has been verified by their family members, legal documents and newspaper articles. The participation of others has not. Without family verification, court records or newspaper articles, suspected individuals are not herein mentioned.

The most unique thing I have heard about the Yates family's manufacturing is that they did not use wood or coal for their heat source. There were gas lines that crossed

Grandma's property and her family tapped into them for their distillation heat source. Arrangements were made with employees from the gas company and those employees were rewarded with product and cash. Since revenuers were known to spot stills by an area of chopped trees, the smoke, flames and smell from the wood fires in secluded areas, it was far more difficult for the Yates/Delawder family to be found, as they were using an odorless natural gas flame. They also used different sites of the two-hundred-acre property and even had one still on Great-uncle Ike's property. When cousins, neighbors, and in-laws participated, the locations were numerous.

Therefore, I don't believe my family was involved in an organized ring. I believe it was a family manufacturing business, or distillation business with the aid and support of neighbors and in-laws.

I have also been told my grandmother was an active participant by folks who bought their shine directly from her and from others who purchased theirs from her sons and brothers. There is also documented proof of her involvement.

In addition to the manufacturing of distilled liquor, Grandma and her sons managed a two-hundred-acre property, milked cows, and raised livestock, crops, and children. When the weather was too hot or too cold for manufacturing, the men traveled to other parts of the state to pick, husk and shock corn. They sold, butchered and cured their meat, walked to church, helped their neighbors, and transported their mother and younger siblings wherever they needed to go.

Information is difficult to obtain today from incidents that happened in the 1920's and 30's, but I have learned where six of the Yates stills were located. The first one mentioned in the indictment was Uncle Marion's still on the Jonah Main farm in Delaware County. This property was located via a 1940 article in *The Marion Star* regarding a William Glenn, who died during a fire in a cabin he rented from Jonah Main that was located "two miles west of Leonardsburg, south of Ashley". Another of the Yates stills was located on the border of the Yates/Kelly (Preacher James Thomas Kelly and his sixteen children) property up a hollow off of Elkins Creek in Aid Township. There was also a still up the hollow across from Grandma's house (now federally-owned land) where the barn Uncle Forrest built now stands. The Yates boys took the liberty of setting up another still in the hollow behind Great-uncle Ike's house. My favorite Yates still location, and the one most commonly known, was on top of the cave called the rock house, located on the left of the Five Forks Hill headed downward toward Elkins Creek. It was the most accessible to traffic and customers. The last known still was not in Lawrence County and its location remains a family secret. In addition to the Yates stills, there were also Delawder stills; two near Cannons Creek were previously mentioned on page 45, just prior to the Delawder brothers photo, in an Ironton newspaper article dated October 25, 1923.

A Yates family still was located on the hill above the rock house cave. Great-uncle Hobart Delawder was arrested at this site.

A Yates still was located in the hollow beyond and to the left of the above barn Uncle Forrest built around 1950.

An Ironton resident and a distant cousin told me recently people liked buying from the Yates family because: they were not greedy; Grandma was a fine, respected woman; the family was honest and hardworking; they didn't allow people around their property and business drinking, fighting or causing trouble; the whisky was of the finest quality; and the product was delivered.

A few folks in their eighties and nineties have been wonderful resources, along with several other younger folks; but only one person who has furnished information to me, my cousin Norman Humphrey, has ever seen the infamous Revenuer Coach, a fellow who is discussed in the next chapter.

Chapter 6

Revenuers and Lawmen

"What's in a name? That which we call a rose by any other name would smell as sweet." (Shakespeare's "Romeo and Juliet")

From the above quote, one could deduce, that by any other name, revenuers would be the same.

According to Wiktionary, "a revenuer is an employee of the IRS, especially those charged with enforcement". This term first came into use during the Prohibition Era and stuck around even after the 21st Amendment to the United States Constitution.

During the Prohibition Era the folks in New Straitsville, Ohio, according to their book, *Our Journey Continues,* called the men from the IRS looking for moonshiners "dry dicks".

On The Blue Ridge Institute's website's list of moonshine-related definitions, the cost paid to law enforcement officers who took bribes or payoff money was called a "granny fee". In Lawrence County, federal revenuers and local officials were rumored to collect protection, or "granny fees". There were also some in southern Ohio who were not just rumored, but caught by the feds.

An article in *The Ironton Tribune* in May of 1932 explained how U.S. Department of Justice inspectors worked their way into the confidence of a certain group of distillers in Chesapeake, Lawrence County, Ohio, and became members as "part of a plot worked by federal agents to entrap" some crooked local officers who were charging protection fees and collecting profits from illegal sales.

An article in *The Ironton Tribune* dated April 11, 1932, stated Orville Carson, the marshal of Proctorville, Lawrence County, Ohio, and his deputy, Meldon A. Neff "solicited and accepted bribes from distillers". Another article included Ben Dunfee, constable of Windsor Township, along with Carson and Neff stating, "The three officers are now in the Scioto County Jail at Portsmouth having failed to provide $10,000 bail."

Seemingly some folks thought the local authorities in southern Ohio gave those arrested for liquor offenses too much leeway, so the Prosecutor in Portsmouth decided to refer them to someone who would not be so lenient, the federal courts. An October 25, 1923, article from the *Portsmouth Daily Times* stated,

> "At Prosecutor Elkins' office it was announced that those convicted of liquor offenses have in many cases employed every tactic and technicality possible to secure delay in execution of sentences pronounced, by appeal and otherwise, that it was now deemed advisable to eliminate these in part, by taking such cases to the federal court."

The *Encyclopedia of Appalachia* states,

> "The mid-1960's witnessed Operation Dry-Up, a massive campaign against moonshiners. Although the conflict between revenuers (now the Bureau of Alcohol, Tobacco, Firearms, and

Explosives, a division of the Department of Justice) and moonshiners has not abated".

So, according to the above-mentioned encyclopedia, revenuers with different department names and officer titles still smell and/or are the same to the moonshiners.

Verbal folk history, TV shows like "The Dukes of Hazzard" and Hollywood movies make the moonshiners into heroes and the revenuers into the bad guys. Surely there must be reasons for this, perhaps federal agents like Evans Barnett mentioned in Chapter 4.

In today's world, what were once called revenuers with the Internal Revenue Service now are called ATF agents and are employed through the Bureau of Alcohol, Tobacco, Firearms, and Explosives. From the department's website, the following brief history is provided:

> "Effective January 24, 2003, the Bureau of Alcohol, Tobacco, Firearms and Explosives (ATF) was transferred under the Homeland Security bill to the Department of Justice. The law enforcement functions of the ATF under the Department of the Treasury were transferred to the Department of Justice. The tax and trade functions of ATF will remain in the Treasury Department with the new Alcohol and Tobacco Tax Trade Bureau. In addition, the agency's name was changed to the Bureau of Alcohol, Tobacco, Firearms and Explosives (ATF) to reflect its new mission in the Department of Justice".

The agency's website includes a brief history from Oxford University Press from 1789–1998, describing ATF as a tax-collecting, enforcement and regulatory agency of the U.S Department of the Treasury. The department's responsibility is regulated by Congress and the department cannot make or amend the laws it has to follow. The department further claims,

> "professional neutrality while giving a 35 – 1 return on every dollar it spends. ATF has the best cost-to-collection ratio in the federal family."

The website depicts ATF as "the youngest tax-collecting Treasury agency," and states ATF is separated from the IRS by Treasury Department Order No. 120-1, which was effective July 1, 1972. "Not withstanding, ATF traces its roots across two hundred years of American history."

The Alcohol and Tobacco Tax and Trade Bureau of the U.S. Department of the Treasury also has a website. In the revised 0406 FAQs one can learn it is legal for an individual eighteen years of age or above to make up to one hundred gallons of beer or wine for one's own use or up to two hundred gallons for a family's use without paying federal excise tax and filing paperwork. However,

> "You cannot produce spirits for beverage purposes without paying taxes and without prior approval of paperwork to operate a distilled spirits plant (See 26 U.S. C. 5601 & 5602 for some of the criminal penalties.) There are numerous requirements that must be met that make it impractical to produce spirits for personal or beverage use. Some of these re-

quirements are paying excise tax, filing an extensive application, filing a bond, providing adequate equipment to measure spirits, providing suitable tanks and pipelines, providing a separate building (other than a dwelling) and maintaining detailed records, and filing reports. All of these requirements are listed in 27 CFR Part 19."

The special Operations Division of the ATF, as per a chart on their website, seized 86,416 gallons of illicit spirits in 1970, 16,046 in 1975, none in 1980, 218 in 1985, 4 in 1990, and 1,600 in 1995. The facts depict a current increase in gallons being seized, and possibly indicate a trend and increase in production.

If a person wants some 'shine today, it's not difficult to find. However, since it is illegal to make spirits, or moonshine, as a beverage for one's personal use under any circumstances (there are some complicated ways to get government approval), I refuse to tell any of the wonderful stories I have been told (none in writing) that might implicate anyone living today in a federal crime. Nor have I kept notes that could be used against anyone.

Some have told me they are current distillers and actually have given me verbal permission to include them in this publication, but I choose not to do so.

Without having seen the actual working still, I have no proof one exists. Besides, I don't want anyone to ever end up in jail from information published in one of my books.

Some folks have told me about making moonshine on their own property for their own use many decades ago.

Others have told me of those who made it for sale. As recently as 2005, Mom sent my sister Shirley and me out into the country hills of Lawrence County to buy home-manufactured spirits for her. (After her morning coffee, moonshine was Mom's favorite drink.) She sipped moonshine and beer from a covered coffee mug and few people ever knew she partook of alcohol at all.

Fortunately, for the sake of the distillers, Shirley (now also deceased) was driving and I don't remember the directions, locations or names of the distillers. If I had remembered, I would have contacted them to get their permission to take some photographs of their stills for this publication.

Various gals from the hills have told me personal secrets about first dates (with their now husbands) many years ago and how moonshine was involved. Some friends have told me of relatives who were dry officers or officers of the law. They too had some interesting stories to share.

As mentioned earlier, my great-uncle Ray Thornton was a law officer in Lawrence and Cuyahoga Counties. The 1930 Lawrence County, Upper Township, Census Record listed his occupation as a Prohibition Inspector. He died in 1958 in Lakewood, Cuyahoga County, Ohio. He was respected, even by those he arrested. Some of the criminals he dealt with have told me what a good police officer he was when they connected my maiden name of Thornton with his. One was a murderer. As she talked with me in her kitchen, she was hacking on her oak table with a butcher knife, which frightened me at the time, because I was her social worker and knew she had actually stabbed two different men to death. While she continued chopping that knife into the wood, she told me if it hadn't been for the goodness of Ray Thornton she would have been executed. She laughed loudly and told me she was having fun with me. From that moment on, we had a great client/professsional relationship.

Ray Thornton as a young man

There were many honest revenuers and law enforcement officers during Prohibition and there are many honest law enforcement officers now, but unfortunately they aren't the ones we hear much about.

Daniel Hieronimus, a former Kitts Hill and Rock Hill schoolmate, was an honest Ohio Highway Patrolman and

Lawrence County Sheriff. During his time in office as sheriff of Lawrence County, the crime rate there was reduced by approximately 40% even though his budget was 26% less than that of the previous sheriff. Dan implemented youth development and crime prevention programs rather than just arresting criminals. He was instrumental in starting air shows to raise over $200,000 through corporate sponsors to contribute to youth development and involved the youth in the air shows as well.

David Carmon, a former Rock Hill classmate and good student, was an honest Ohio Highway Patrolman. He and his wife Dora now live in Wheelersburg.

Sergeant John (Jack) S. Jones, an uncle by marriage and an Ohio Highway Patrolman, was an excellent lawman and a wonderful person. He was commander of the South Point post for many years, beginning during my childhood. After retiring from the Ohio Highway Patrol, he served as an investigator for the Jackson County Prosecutor's Office.

Dan Greene, an Ohio Highway Patrolman, was raised in a wonderful family in Albany, Athens County, Ohio, to be honest and dependable. He too served at the South Point post. Dan was a young boy when I was in college and his older brother, Randy, was a good friend of mine.

Emmett McIntyre, a Lawrence County native, served with the Ohio Highway Patrol from 1954 to 1959. He served under Post Commander John S. Jones. When I was a child, Emmett lived on the same road I did. He is also a first cousin of my older brother's widow.

Lewis McKee, the Chief of Police in South Point, Ohio, during my childhood, and a paternal uncle, was honest and respected. Following his retirement, he and Aunt Marie spent much more of their time in Florida.

Lewis McKee served as Chief of Police in South Point, Ohio, around the 1950's.

The above photo of Jack Jones was taken around the time he was employed by the Jackson County Prosecutor.

David Carmon served with
the Ohio Highway Patrol around
the late 1960's and/or early 1970's.

Daniel Hieronimus

Daniel Hieronimus served as an Ohio Highway Patrolman from 1971 to 1981.

Dan Hieronimus served as Lawrence County Sheriff from 1981 to 1992.

The above photo is of a confiscated still and dry officers in Lawrence County, Ohio. The photo was contributed by Marta Sutton Ramey at Briggs Library and was probably from an I*ronton Tribune* article. The only person identified is Andrew Washington, the third man from the left.

Some folks have told me of secret family stills in various places in the past, but don't want their secrets revealed. One gal from Huron, Ohio, (I met her at a Wendy's in Bucyrus this past May) told me she currently has a still in her garage.

There are all types of small business transactions taking place without proper government forms being completed or proper income taxes being paid, yet for some reason our government is biased against those who make moonshine.

There are various fiscal entities, including flea markets, craft shows, yard sales, grooming and dog-watching, art shows, vending at festivals, home sewing for hire, baby-sitting, house painting and lawn care servicing (to name only a few), that operate without a vendor's license and don't pay taxes on their profits. People gladly pay for these services and turn "a blind eye" to the income tax evasion and "under the table" transactions. Such behavior is even common in Congress and churches. Yet, it is a federal crime to make spirits for one's own use, largely because of whisky taxes. It hardly seems fair. Situations such as these contribute to why the moonshiners have become the folk heroes and the revenuers have become the bad guys. Tax revenue or money is the issue, not the moonshine.

The Department of the Treasury, Alcohol and Tobacco Tax and Trade Bureau Statistical Report - Distilled Spirits for the reporting period of the year 2010 on their website indicates 75,305,814 gallons of whisky were made in the U.S. in 2009 and 83,392,376 were made in 2010. There was far less brandy, rum, gin and vodka made. Imports are not included in these figures. Think of the tax dollars the U.S Treasury Department makes each year on whisky alone. It is no wonder that Uncle Sam doesn't want individuals making any for their own use. It's all about money. There is no way national security is endangered by whisky of any kind in comparison to terrorists with firearms and explosives.

Teachers and schools can file papers and get permission to make whisky in classes. If it is too dangerous to do legally in our homes, why in the world would it be safe and legal in schools full of hundreds of children?

We made whisky in the chemistry lab at Ironton High School when I was a student. Making whisky is a part of Lawrence County's and Appalachia's culture. Why is it not legal to make in the privacy and safety of one's home? Obviously, there is some good in teaching and learning the process. Why else would it be permitted?

If it were actually a safety hazard, then why would the Bureau of Alcohol, Tobacco, Firearms and Explosives permit it to be made at a festival where thousands of people are roaming the streets?

Even food is harmful if too much of it is eaten. There are licensed medications taken off the market by the FDA because of harmful effects. I have had negative reactions to numerous medications, yet not one time did I ever get ill effects from the hot toddies my grandmother Thornton made to treat coughs and colds. Again, drugs are big business and contribute to the Treasury's coffers. This too makes the tax collectors and revenuers lose favor with the public.

It seems tax collectors have been ill thought of for centuries. In the *King James Scofield Study Bible,* Luke 19:1-10 tells the story of Zacchaeus, a rich sinner, footnoted to be described as a "crooked tax collector". He sought forgiveness with the intention of:

> "Half of my goods I give to the poor; and if I have taken any thing from any man by false accusation, I will restore him fourfold.";

and Jesus forgave him.

In today's cruel, greedy world, it wouldn't be difficult to imagine our Sweet Jesus being snitched out and arrested for income tax evasion or for violating liquor laws because of his first miracle in Cana.

I don't know that Revenuer Coach ever sought forgiveness from Jesus Christ. I have searched the web and available records trying to find information about this fellow named "Coach". There doesn't seem to be any written documentation readily available to confirm the man ever existed. There was a James Coach listed in the 1939 *Ironton City Directory* and a couple more men with the last name of Coach mentioned in the *Huntington City Directory* in the late 1930's, but no indication that any of them was an IRS employee. Officer Coach was a legend in his own lifetime, for being an "asshole" instead of for the good he did. He did not and still does not have a good reputation. I have heard far worse things said about him than of the people he sought out for the manufacture of unregistered whisky.

I have been told (by several people) how Coach frequently stopped my grandmother on her way to and from her home to taunt her by telling her he wanted to look at her eggs.

He would say things like, "Nice eggs, Miss Yates. Now let me see what's in the trunk of your car."

He followed her into the grocery store to try to embarrass her. He checked with grocers about her purchases to try to prove she was buying products to make whisky. Not one time did he ever catch her doing anything illegal, yet he constantly tormented her.

It has been reported to me he also taunted my uncles. They didn't mind so much, as they were manufacturing whisky. They would laughingly tell stories about Coach chasing them through the woods firing shots at them and following them in automobiles on the dirt roads of Lawrence County.

Agent Coach reportedly harassed young Uncle Ike at the courthouse to make him angry in hopes of provoking him to violence in order to increase charges against him. He is said to have accused Lem Waugh of having a still outside his kitchen door, but other officers of the law refuted his statements. He also accused Lem of being responsible for other offenses of which he was exonerated.

On another occasion, Coach learned Marion Yates, along with some of his brothers and in-laws, was picking corn in Clark County, Ohio. He contacted the Clark County Sheriff and told him where the men were picking and staying on the property in a log cabin. He proceeded to advise the Sheriff the men were armed and dangerous and asked him to arrest Uncle Marion. During the night, as the men were resting after a long day of labor picking corn, cutting stalks and shocking fodder, Uncle Marion awakened and went outside the cabin to take a leak. He was standing facing some woods with his pants down and his back facing the rear of the cabin when he was told to "drop your weapon." It was said he wasn't even given the opportunity to pull up his pants before being cuffed. The cabin was searched and only corn knives and picking gloves were found. Reportedly Coach tried desperately to admit the corn knives and gloves as weapons to the court, to the embarrassment of the arresting sheriff.

In another reported incident on a hot, muggy day, Revenuer Coach was out chasing still manufacturers. During the chase he got hot, sweaty and thirsty. He went into a private home near the still with some of his helpers to beg a drink of cool water. Inside the house was a visitor, the son of a man Coach had been trying to trap for some time. After finishing his drink, Coach arrested the young man for fleeing arrest. Coach's coworkers told him in front of the homeowner's family that this young man could not have been fleeing, as they had run quite a distance through the woods and that this young man was not sweaty or dirty. Coach arrested and charged him anyway. When the case went to court, the judge listened to the young man's plea along with the statements of Coach's peers and dismissed all charges against the boy, much to Coach's dismay and embarrassment. In retaliation Coach continued to harass the young fellow for years.

Another incident told to me involving "bad guy" Coach is in relation to a moonshiner by the name of Jim Pinkerman. Seemingly Pinkerman moved away from Lawrence County to keep his manufacturing business going without getting himself arrested. He headed south. Coach did the same and they ended up in the same state. Eventually Coach got so greedy he was taking bribes as protection money from manufacturers and got caught for his fraudulent activities. Folks were glad he finally got what he deserved. However I have not been able to verify this story because I have been unable to even learn Coach's first name.

Harold Yates, my cousin, recently told me a story about his Uncle Johnny Waugh being shot in the early 1930's as he and some of his siblings and friends were walking home from church. The bullet went into his side, scaring all those with him. Johnny, seriously injured and treated by ole Doc Hunter, recovered from the wound, but the bullet could not be found. Years later it worked its way out of his hip. Some folks thought the revenuers might have been who shot John. Others thought it might have something to do with a fellow being jealous of pretty Cora Waugh,

Johnny's sister, and thinking she was being escorted home by a romantic interest, mistaking Johnny for someone else. The person who shot him with a .22 caliber was never identified or caught.

Who shot John was indeed a mystery, but folks figured it might have something to do with the family business because revenuers were known to shoot at folks back then.

It was also known that Coach had a vendetta against Lem Waugh, Johnny's dad. It's easy to understand why the federal agent was suspected, as Johnny's brother, Otis, was one who had been fired upon by revenuers so many times he decided to get out and stay out of moonshining. However, no one expected a "feller" to get fired upon while on the way home from a church.

When young men went missing in the hills and never turned up, foul play and a regretful end were the grief of manufacturing families and Coach was the number one cold-blooded suspect. I've not heard of anyone ever firing at Coach.

Folks have told me it was a good thing computers and photo-editing programs were not around in Coach's time, as he took lots of photos as evidence and would have surely altered them to frame innocent folks if he could have.

Coach had quite a reputation. Fortunately the local law officers were not looked upon with such disdain. To folks who recall his presence, Coach is now no more than a bad memory.

The one person still alive who remembers seeing Agent Coach is Norman Humphrey. Norman, at the time a child of about seven, saw him once in the Lawrence County Courthouse when his grandma's and uncles' cases were being heard. Norman described the agent as a man of medium height, stern countenance, and stocky build; yet because of Coach's spiteful demeanor, Norman never noticed his hair color, if he were bald, or if he wore glasses. Seeing Coach was an unpleasant experience for a child.

Thus, because of Coach and others like him, revenuers took first place as the bad guys. The manufacturers were just good ole country boys, working hard at trying to make a living for themselves and their large families during tough times. They provided a desired service to appreciative customers.

Coach was persistent and this quality, along with his seemingly innate drive, led him to numerous arrests you'll learn about in the next chapter.

Chapter 7

Federal Court Proceedings

Except for the last two paragraphs, which summarize the sentencing documentation of both counts, this chapter is a direct quote from case number 5555, filed in the October Term in the year nineteen hundred and thirty-nine of the Southern District of Ohio, Western Division by Harry F. Rabe, Clerk.

The case reads as follows:

"FIRST COUNT:

Section 88,
Title 18,
United States Code.

The Grand Jurors of the United States of America, empanelled and sworn in the District Court of the United States for the Western Division of the Southern Judicial District of Ohio, at the October Term thereof, in the year nineteen hundred and thirty-nine, and inquiring for that division and district, upon their oaths and affirmations present:

That:

PAUL LEGG

MARION R. YATES

FORREST YATES

EARL YATES

CORA YATES

HOBART M. DELAWDER

HARLIN [sic] E. WAUGH

RAYMOND DELONG,

THOMAS DELONG, and

THOMAS G. KELLY,

Hereinafter referred to as defendants, and

Marvin J. Siders

Paul Johnson, and

Willard Waugh,

co-conspirators but not defendants herein, and divers other persons to these Grand

Jurors unknown, from on or about the first day of February, in the year nineteen hundred and thirty-seven, and thence continuously up to and including the date of the returning of this indictment, in the Counties of Delaware and Lawrence, State of Ohio, within the Western Division of the Southern Judicial District of Ohio, and within the jurisdiction of this Court, unlawfully, knowingly, willfully and feloniously did conspire, combine, confederate and agree together, each with the other and with divers other persons to this Grand Jury unknown, to commit divers offenses against the United States of America, to-wit, unlawfully to violate Section 1152 (a), Title 26, United States code Annotated; Section 1162, Title 26, United States Code Annotated; Section 1184, Title 26, United States Code Annotated; that is to say, the said defendants and co-conspirators did conspire, combine, confederate and agree together, each with the other and with divers other persons to these Grand Jurors unknown, to buy, sell, transport and have in their possession and under their control quantities of distilled spirits without having affixed to each of the immediate containers thereof, stamps denoting the quantity of distilled spirits contained therein, said stamps evidencing payment of all internal revenue taxes imposed on said distilled spirits, by law, to have in their possession and custody and under their control, stills and distilling apparatus set up for the production of spirituous liquors without having the same registered as required by law, to carry on the business of distillers without having given bond as required by law, and with intent to defraud the United States of the taxes on the spirits distilled by them and to make and ferment in large quantities in amounts to these Grand Jurors unknown, mash fit for distillation, in buildings and upon certain premises other than distilleries authorized by law.

OVERT ACTS

And the Grand Jurors aforesaid, upon their oaths and affirmations aforesaid, do say that in furtherance of said unlawful agreement, combination and conspiracy, and for purpose of accomplishing said unlawful purpose as hereinbefore charged, the said defendants, at the times and places hereinafter set forth, did commit the following overt acts, to-wit:

1. On February 1, 1937 and continuously to April 22, 1937, PAUL LEGG and MARION R. YATES, defendants, had in their possession and under their control an unregistered still of three hundred (300)

gallons capacity, set up, on the farm of Jonah Main in Delaware County, Ohio.

2. On September 14, 1937, THOMAS DELONG, defendant, had in his possession and under his control, an unregistered still of sixty (60) gallons capacity, set up, and operated by him in Lawrence County, Ohio.

3. On November 27, 1937, MARION R. YATES and FORREST YATES, defendants, sold and delivered to Marvin J. Siders, co-conspirator, twenty (20) gallons of tax-unpaid whiskey at the home of CORA YATES, defendant, in Lawrence County, Ohio.

4. From January to March, 1938, PAUL LEGG, MARION R. YATES, FORREST YATES and EARL YATES, defendants, had in their possession and under their control, near the home of CORA YATES, defendant, in Lawrence County, Ohio, an unregistered still of one hundred eighty (180) gallons capacity, set up.

5. On February 5, 1938, FORREST YATES and PAUL LEGG, defendants, purchased, in the name of John Delawder, six (6) pounds of yeast and six hundred (600) pounds of sugar from C.H. Keeney of the

Keeney Grocery Company, Ironton, Ohio, this yeast being delivered to a car bearing license number P-2594 issued to PAUL LEGG.

6. On February 10, 1938, RAYMOND DELONG, defendant, purchased from Amos Keeney, of the Keeney Grocery Company in Ironton, Ohio, sixteen (16) pounds of yeast for the sum of $4.80.

7. On February 25, 1938, RAYMOND DELONG and THOMAS DELONG, defendants, transported ten (10) gallons of tax-unpaid whiskey over the public highways of Lawrence County, Ohio.

8. On March 4, 1938, FORREST YATES and EARL YATES, defendants, operated an unregistered still of one hundred eighty (180) gallons capacity and manufactured sixty-one (61) gallons of tax-unpaid whiskey near the home of CORA YATES, defendant, in Lawrence County, Ohio.

9. In the later part of March, 1938, RAYMOND and THOMAS DELONG, defendants, had in their possession and under their control, an unregistered still in Lawrence County, Ohio, which they operated.

10. In March, 1938, PAUL LEGG, MARION R. YATES and HARLIN [sic] E.WAUGH, defendants, set up an unregistered still of four hundred (400) gallons capacity near the home of Harlin [sic] Waugh, in Lawrence County, Ohio, and had some in their possession and under their control continuously until July 11, 1938.

11. On October 17, 1938, PAUL LEGG, RAYMOND DELONG, and EARL YATES, defendants, operated an unregistered still of two hundred and seventy (270) gallons capacity in Aid Township, Lawrence County, Ohio, said EARL YATES blowing a horn as warning for said PAUL LEGG and RAYMOND DELONG to escape from this still.

12. In December 1938, HARLIN [sic] E. WAUGH and MARION R. YATES, defendants, set up an unregistered still of one hundred twenty (120) gallons capacity and had same in their possession and under their control until March, 1939, in Aid Township, Lawrence County, Ohio.

13. In January 1939, PAUL LEGG and FORREST YATES, defendants, made several purchases of sugar from Charles Steed at Kroger's Grocery in Ironton, Ohio, said sugar being delivered to a car bearing license number Z-356-P which was registered in the name of PAUL LEGG.

14. In February, 1939, HOBART M. DELAWDER, defendant, had in his possession and under his control an unregistered still of sixty (60) gallons capacity near the home of CORA YATES, defendant, Lawrence County, Ohio.

15. About February 15, 1939, THOMAS G. KELLY, defendant, borrowed $7.00 from PAUL LEGG, defendant, in Lawrence County, Ohio.

16. On March 13, 1939, on the farm of CORA YATES, defendant, FORREST YATES and EARL YATES, defendants, had in their possession and under their control an unregistered still of (60) gallons capacity.

17. On March 13, 1939, PAUL LEGG, MARION YATES and HARLIN [sic] E. WAUGH, defendants, purchased from Wain [sic] Kelly at the Hannan Grocery Company, Ironton, Ohio, one

hundred (100) pounds of bran for use in compounding of whiskey mash.

18. On March 13, 1939, at the home of CORA YATES, defendant, in Lawrence County, Ohio, PAUL LEGG, MARION R.YATES, HARLIN [sic] E.WAUGH, FOR-REST YATES, EARL YATES and HOBART M. DELAWDER, defendants, congregated and held conversations, each with the other.

19. On March 14, 1939, PAUL LEGG, HOBART M. DELAWDER and THOMAS G. KELLY, defendants, operated an unregistered still of two hundred seventy-two (272) gallons capacity, near the home of CORA YATES, defendant, in Lawrence County, Ohio.

20. On March 14, 1939, CORA YATES, FORREST YATES and EARL YATES, defendants, at their home in Lawrence County, Ohio, had in their possession two hundred (200) pounds of charcoal, twenty-three (23) one-gallon jugs, two (2) five-gallon cans, and other materials and utensils commonly used in the compounding of mash and the operation of unregistered stills.

CONCLUSION

And so the Grand Jurors aforesaid, upon their oaths and affirmations aforesaid, do say that said defendants, throughout the period of time, and in place, manner and form aforesaid, unlawfully and feloniously did conspire to commit offense against the United States and did do acts to effect the objects of the conspiracy:

Contrary to the form of the statute in such case made and provided and against the peace and dignity of the United States of America.

Second Count:
Section 1152 (a.), Title 26, United States Code Annotated.

And the Grand Jurors aforesaid upon their oaths and affirmations Aforesaid, do further present:

That

PAUL LEGG

MARION R. YATES

FORREST YATES

EARL YATES

CORA YATES

HOBART M. DELAWDER

HARLIN [sic] E. WAUGH

RAYMOND DELONG

THOMAS DELONG, and

THOMAS G. KELLY,

and divers other persons to these Grand Jurors unknown, from on or about the first day of February, in the year nineteen hundred and thirty-seven, and thence continuously up to and including the date of the returning of this indictment, in the Counties of Delaware and Lawrence, State of Ohio, within the Western Division of the Southern Judicial District of Ohio, and within the jurisdiction of this Court, did knowingly, willfully, unlawfully, and feloniously buy, sell, transport, and have in their possession and under their control quantities of distilled spirits without having affixed to each of the immediate containers thereof, stamps denoting the quantity of distilled spirits contained therein, said stamps evidencing payment of all internal revenue taxes imposed on said distilled spirits by law, in violation of Section 1152 (a), Title 26, United States Code Annotated; contrary to the form of the statute in such case made and provided, and against the peace and dignity of the United States of America."

All defendants pled guilty of the two charges. Cora Yates had both counts suspended and was placed on probations for said periods of time, two years and six months. Hobart M. Delawder was sentenced to four months on count one and the two years on count two were suspended and he was placed on probation for two years on count two of the indictment. Raymond Delong had both counts suspended and was placed on probation for six months. Thomas Delong was sentenced to six months on count one and count two was suspended and he was placed on probation for two years. Thomas G. Kelly received four months in the penitentiary on count one and count two was suspended and defendant placed on probation for two years. Paul Legg was sentenced to fifteen months on count one and count two was suspended with two years probation. Harlan E. Waugh was sentenced to four months on count one and received two years, suspended and placed on two years probation for count two. Earl Yates received six months on count one and had a two-year suspended sentence with two years of probation for count two. Forrest Yates received six months on count one and two years suspended with two years probation on count two. Marion Yates was sentenced to one year and one day on count one and received a two-year sentence on count two, suspended and defendant placed on probation for the said two years.

There is no sentencing information on the co-defendants, Marvin J. Siders, Paul Johnson, and Willard Waugh.

Chapter 8

Commentary on Court Proceedings

The numbered items that follow are to be referenced to the item of the same number in Chapter 7.

Item 1. I have yet to make contact with Paul Legg or any of his heirs. I did locate a great-nephew, Chuck, who went to grade school with me and had heard talk about Paul being involved in moonshining, but knew no details of the incidents, nor did he know much about Paul Legg. The Delaware County Historical Society had no information on Paul Legg or Jonah Main, but did refer me to the Delaware County Genealogical Society. The Genealogical Society sent me a copy of a Delaware County, Ohio, Probate Court Journal Entry on Arraignment, case number 11091, dated September 26, 1926, and a Warrant to Arrest, charging Paul Legg with illegal possession – Intoxicating Liquor. Paul signed the documents as H. Paul Legg. He was found guilty and adjudged to pay a fine of one thousand dollars. A Lee Main entered into a recognizance for him. Legg was released when his wife came for him. Records indicate H. Paul Legg and Paul H. Legg are one and the same person. Paul later moved to Lawrence County, was a court-documented associate of my uncles and grandmother and was last known by Harley Vanmeter, a family friend, to live in Ironton.

There was an article in a 1940 edition of the *Marion Star* verifying the fact Jonah Main did own a farm in

Delaware County near Ashley. He was no doubt related to the aforementioned Lee Main, and possibly was Lee Main.

Item 2. I have yet to make contact with descendents of Thomas Delong. However I have talked with some of his cousins and nephews who are aware of his involvement in the illegal distillation business.

Item 3. Descendants of Marion R. Yates and Forrest Yates have been very cooperative. Phone calls and a visit were made to the son of Marvin J. Siders and phone calls have been made to his grandson, all to no avail.

Item 4. My comment to this 180 gallon still and item 1 (300 gallon still), item 8 (180 gallon still), item 10 (400 gallon still), item 11 (270 gallon still) and item 19 (272 gallon still) is that the officers mentioned in the newspaper article of "Enormous Still" on page 34 (still estimated to hold 165 gallons) hadn't really seen much in the way of enormous stills compared with the ones my family used.

Items 5 & 6. John Delawder was another of Grandma's brothers. He lived in Illinois prior to the 1930's, as verified by the article about the death of Homer Delawder mentioned in Chapter 5, and probably had little or nothing to do with the sugar purchase, unless he was by chance visiting from Illinois at the time. Hannan's Grocery was owned by Thomas S. and Mrs. Alma Kinney and Hugh L Murray and was located in Ironton, Ohio, at 205-207 North 3rd Street. This was verified via an 1882-83 *Ironton City Directory* by Marta Sutton Ramey at Briggs Library in Lawrence County. She found the store continued to be in business far beyond 1938, into my lifetime, but did change addresses. The Keeney Grocery first appeared in the 1940 *Ironton City Directory* under the name of Amos Keeney, a cousin of Marta. Keeney's Grocery was located at 110 South 4th Street. Her recollection of Amos is as a meatcutter for Kroger's.

Item 7. Raymond Delong lived at Kitts Hill, Ohio. No address was given for Thomas Delong, but both were raised on Rucker Ridge, near the Yates home. They would have had to use the public roads to get from their brotherly home on Rucker Ridge to Kitts Hill in a car. The Keeney Grocery Store is verified in Item 5 above. When I was a child, Thomas Delong lived on the same road as my family, but closer to the intersection of Homeless Road. Tom lived up the hollow on the left just before reaching the intersection of Little Sharps Creek, which we called Buck Creek, and Homeless Road near the Lawrence Harper residence.

Now all of the roads are numbered and the old names are no longer used.

There is no other information to substantiate or refute this item, other than Thomas and Raymond were brothers. They had a married sister who also lived at Kitts Hill on the same road I did as a child.

Item 8. I am aware of six different stills operated by the Yates/Delawder family, as discussed in Chapter 4. There were probably more I don't know about since Great–uncles Homer and Albert Delawder were involved prior to the birth of my mother. Subsequent to marrying and leaving the home of their mother, widow Lydia Delawder, both resided on Elkins Creek. Oak Ridge Furnace was, at one time, located on property owned by the Delawder family. I do not know the exact location of Great-uncle Albert's home. Great-uncle Charley Yates also had a still on his property on Aarons Creek.

The above photo is of my Dad, Bill Thornton, at the rock house cave sometime around 1939. Wonder what that is he's holding in the hand against his hip?

As children Phillip Boggs and I (and sometimes our brothers) roamed the hills and dales around his home (the Preacher James Thomas Kelly property) and Grandma's property and found some old pieces of metal and glass that were probably once part of the still in the hollow across from the Yates home, behind Uncle Forrest's barn.

Shown above are: Billy Thornton, Ronnie Thornton (my brothers) and Phillip Boggs beside my Grandma's house around 1956.

Item 9. I have no further information about the Delongs.

Harlan E. Waugh in the early
1940's in his WW II Army uniform

Item 10. Harlan Waugh married Mom's first cousin, Dorothy Delawder, daughter of Albert and Nettie Leffingwell Delawder. Marion Yates married Harlan's and Willard's sister, Ida Waugh. Harlan's daughter, Phyllis Clary, remembers hearing family moonshine stories, but was not aware her father and grandfather, Albert Delawder, had actually been arrested or that her father had served time, until the copy of her dad's indictment was sent to me and the article about her grandfather was recently found in the 1926 Portsmouth newspaper.

Harlan's name was misspelled as "Harlin" in the court records in Chapter 7.

Willard Waugh long after his moonshining days

Item 11. I have yet to figure out the connection with Paul Legg because I cannot locate his heirs. However, a Paul H. Legg was found in a 1939 Delaware, Ohio, City Directory via ancestry.com. It was verified that he was arrested in Delaware County for a moonshine-related charge. He later moved to Lawrence County, Ohio, was known to be a friend of my uncles (verified in the indictment) and lived the latter part of his life in Ironton.

As stated in the federal indictment (page 102), Uncle Earl blew a horn as a warning. The horn was a conch shell and was kept as a souvenir at the Yates home for many years. Cousin Norman can remember it being around Grandma's dining room when he was a child in the 1940's.

Item 12. Again, Harlan Waugh and Marion Yates were brothers-in-law. Willard Waugh is Harlan's brother. Harlan received time via the 1939 indictment. Willard Waugh, Marvin Siders and Paul Johnson did not. However Paul Johnson was sentenced several years later when I was in grade school.

Item 13. I never realized the Kroger Company was around during the 1930's. I am familiar with the Steed family at Pedro. There is a photo of one of the Steed girls in my *Appalachian Childhood*.

Item 14. Great-uncle Hobart Delawder was Grandma's brother. Their other siblings are mentioned previously in Chapter 5 in the newspaper article about the death and obituary of Homer Delawder and in the newspaper articles in Chapter 4 about the arrest and accidental death of Albert Delawder. Uncle Hobart is thought to have lived with Grandma at the time of his arrest.

Item 15. Who would ever think borrowing seven dollars could be used as evidence to send someone to prison? Tommy Kelly, a truly good guy, lived up the hollow past the Yates residence. He married Nola Rucker, daughter of Joe Rucker, Grandma's first cousin and neighbor of

Thomas and Raymond Delong, and also the neighbor of Martha Kimble's family. Tom and Nola lived on the old Ox Road, now called Campbell Drive in Ironton, where Tom built a church in 1957. When the Kelly family moved from Elkins Creek, the Riffits moved in. The Boggs family then moved into the "Preacher Kelly home" a few years after the Riffits moved out.

    Tom's still was not on his dad's property, but up a hollow off of Paddle Creek, commonly called Kimble Hollow.

Thomas G. Kelly in WW II uniform

Item 16. Mom's brothers sure were industrious. It is surprising to me that Uncle Earl was ever so active. Just maybe his heart was stronger than Grandma suspected.

Item 17. Wayne Kelly (misspelled in the indictment as Wain) was Tom Kelly's brother and neighbor of the Cora Yates family. He was fortunate to have had a job at a grocery store during a time when the national economy was at an all-time low.

Item 18. This item amazes me. Heaven forbid Grandma, her sons, her brother, and a nephew-in-law would congregate and hold conversations in her home, each with the other. So what if Paul Legg was visiting there. Grandma always had lots of company. She raised seven children, a grandson, let her bachelor brothers live with her from time to time, had brothers who visited with their families from out-of-state, and she took in occasional boarders to supplement her income from selling eggs, milk and cream.

The above photo of my grandma,
Cora Alice Yates, was taken in 1937.

Item 19. Again, the Kelly property bordered the Yates property. Hobart Delawder lived with his sister, Cora Yates, and her children.

Item 20. The two five-gallon cans were no doubt milk cans. Grandma used them to contain the milk and cream she sold. Since the family used the natural gas lines to fuel their distilleries, it isn't logical they would be buying charcoal, unless it was to char the inside of wooden kegs for the aging process. The charcoal wouldn't be of much help in operating a still, but could have possibly been used as part of the filtering system. The gallon jugs could have been used for numerous purposes: like for cider, milk, juice, or sun tea. Admittedly, one hundred pounds of sugar appears to be an overabundance, but not if canning apple butter or jelly, making syrup or doing a lot of baking. Again, Grandma had seven children, a brother and a grandson living with her. She drank her coffee with so much sugar it was syrupy. Her oatmeal was also overly sweetened. The wheat bran is totally unexplainable, other than as a mash topping, as the Yates family manufactured "liquid corn".

All of the defendants in this case, number 5555, pled guilty. A guilty plea often leads to lesser sentencing.

The co-defendants, Willard Waugh, Paul Johnson, and Marvin Siders were not given a sentence at the time.

Paul Johnson's son, a former Rock Hill School District School Board Member, did not have any photos to contribute because a fire destroyed the family home a few years ago. Paul was sentenced later and served time in a Kentucky Federal Prison during the 1950's, while his son and I attended the then new Rock Hill Elementary School on State Route 141. Hickory Hollow, were he lived, continued through to Hog Run Road, not far from the intersection of State Route 141 near Howard's Grocery (more recently Lambert's Grocery). The son remembered visiting his dad at the prison and that the still was up Hickory Hollow. Paul's grandson, Ricky Johnson, also provided some information. Both young Paul and his son, Ricky, were cooperative.

Willard Waugh never served any time, nor did he discuss his involvement with his sons, Gene or George. Both sons were cooperative. George lives in Marion, Ohio, and Gene lives on the family home place on State Route 141 at Kitts Hill, Ohio. Gene and George both mentioned Otis Waugh, their uncle, and his involvement in the manufacturing and distillation business. He got out of the business because he didn't like getting shot at. A niece, Cora Waugh Thomas (called Corky by the family and in her 70's), relayed an incident of her visiting her grandfather Lem Waugh (the father of Otis, Johnny, Harlan, Willard, and Ida), and hearing gunshots being fired in the distance. At the time she was a small child and was frightened by the noise. She recalled some of the family members stating the shots were probably from revenuers.

It has been reported Johnny Waugh did serve time for moonshining, but I have no documented evidence to verify the report. It has also been suggested Willard and Harlan were present when Marion Yates was arrested in Clark County.

Forrest Yates was arrested in front of Hannan's Grocery Store. His mother was in the store selling eggs at the time of his arrest. She was arrested when she came out of the store because a gallon of moonshine was found in Forrest's vehicle.

Hobart M. Delawder was arrested at the still over the rock house cave. The others got away faster, as Uncle Hobart was a generation older.

Records indicate Earl Yates was not caught. He turned himself in at the Federal Courthouse in Cincinnati while the rest of the family was on trial.

According to Cousin Norman Humphrey, our Uncle Isaac Yates was arrested up the hollow from the Yates home, at the still near the Kelly property line. To date, no record has been found to document this, but Uncle Ike did discuss his involvement with his adult daughters and a son-in-law.

Neither Grandma, nor Mom, ever talked to me about Grandma's involvement, or what the home was like during the trial, prison terms, or probations.

The Yates males stored their product in a trench about two feet deep and approximately one hundred yards long at the foot of the bluff along the base of the hill of the rock house cave, close to the family chicken house. Leaves covered the gallon jugs, insulated and protected them, yet made it easy to uncover the product for delivery and sale.

Harold Yates, older son of Marion, can remember going up the hollow off of the Hog Run Road with his dad in the early 1950's to buy and sell spirits, as Uncle Marion was a friend and co-conspirator of Paul Johnson.

The connection with Jonah Main of Delaware has not yet been determined, but there were members of both the Waugh and Delawder families living within fifteen miles of Johah's farm. Families of customers and other manufacturers from Lawrence County also lived within fifteen miles of Delaware, including Paul Legg, and Ambrose Moore and his son, Edgar. One could assume Jonah Main and Lee Main, both from Delaware County, Ohio, were related, if not one and the same person. There is also documented evidence from court records that Paul Legg was an associate of the Main family, as Lee Main posted bond for Paul's arrest in Delaware County.

There have been other arrests reported by family members of some of the men in the indictment well into my lifetime. Some continued in the manufacturing business into the generation of my children. Some have taught the craft to the young generation of today.

When released from serving time for their crimes, the men known to be moonshiners went on to serve their country in the military, maintained employment, provided well for their families, and led productive lives within their communities.

Thomas G. Kelly obtained donations for the materials and built a Freewill Baptist church on Campbell Drive in Ironton during his spare time, with a little help from some volunteers. There was an article in *The Ironton Tribune* confirming this entitled "The Church That Tom Built" with a photo of Tommy and the church he constructed in 1957-58. There is also information about it on the Campbell Chapel Free Will Baptist Church's website.

Homer Delawder and Albert Delawder are the only suspected business-related fatalities in our family, and both were because of automobile accidents. Both Albert and Homer died in their thirties, leaving behind young widows and small children.

Chapter 9

Other Manufacturers

There have already been numerous southern Ohio residents mentioned in this publication who were active in the manufacturing of illegal spirits. The magnitude of the number of arrests related to the Volstead Act alone is so enormous that not all can be included. Time does not permit me to research all of the residents arrested in even one county, as there were people making moonshine before and after Prohibition. Take for example, in only four 1932 *Ironton Tribune* articles numerous moonshiners who have not been included thus far are: Stanford Smith from Peterstown near Proctorville; Elizabeth Kamer and James Wellman from Chesapeake; Loomis L. Jones from Proctorville; Albert Hampton, Fred Jenkins, LeRoy Johnson, Clarence Abner and James S. Ball, all of Ironton; Carl Henson and Thomas Cunningham from Chesapeake; John Smith, Augusta Smith, Otho Smith, Jacob Sowards, James Holderby, Don Duncan, Elmer Hennington, Herman Holderman, Oscar Smith, Herman W. Bragg, Robert L. Arnold, Bernard Russell Kimble, Turley Gillette, Lafe B. Collins, Lee Collins, Oscar S. "Sim" Bowen, Kenneth Fuller, Stanley Clark, Leroy Smith, John Bowen, Mack McLoughlin and Lou Williams, all just listed as Lawrence County residents with no specific address. Information was given on some of their sentences, but not all. I knew I could not contact every one involved, so had to do some serious thinking.

During a visit to a class on Appalachia at Firelands College in Huron, Ohio, in April of 2011, I had the opportunity to talk with some of the students about my *Appalachian Childhood* and moonshining. Two of about eleven in the class told me they had family members from southern Ohio who were involved in the business. Other students had very interesting questions and comments. I appreciated their remarks and enjoyed the class visit. The professor, Larry Smith, grew up in Appalachia and created a very positive class climate. It was a rewarding educational experience.

On the way home from the class visit I stopped for lunch at a Wendy's in Bucyrus. Two women were in the line ahead of me and as we began to chat I learned they were from Huron and that one of them currently had an active moonshine still in her garage.

During the rest of the trip home I thought about how small the world really is, about the prevalence of moonshine, about my beloved Grandma, my great-uncles, uncles, neighbors and classmates who had or have moonshine connections. I know it is still being made and enjoy hearing the stories of folks past and present.

Before my next speaking engagement, I contacted Lori Kersey and Jennifer Chapman at *The Ironton Tribune* and asked them to include a request for folks in the community to share their moonshine stories and photographs with me for this book. Lori and Jennifer obliged my request and the Lawrence County residents were pleasantly cooperative. The rest of this chapter is about some of their stories.

Several southern Ohio residents have told me about Jim Pinkerman, a Lawrence County native, who was also arrested by IRS Agent Coach. According to multiple reliable sources, Jim served three different prison terms for moonshine-related charges: one in Georgia, one in Pennsylvania and one in Kentucky. Jim finally went to Boxwood, Virginia, in an attempt to get away from Agent Coach's watchful eyes. When the U.S. economy improved, Jim found other employment and provided well for his family.

One of Jim's nephews, George Sanders, told me Jim had approximately seventy people working for his distillation and distributing business. He also stated that the revenuers destroyed so many of the old green and blue Mason jars containing moonshine that there are hardly any of the now antique jars left in the area.

The Pinkermans lived on Paddle Creek, near where my older brother raised his family, and were thought to have stills on both sides of the road. Danny Kitts, who grew up on Paddle Creek during the 1950's and now lives in Marion, Ohio, remembers being told stories about ghosts as a child in order to scare him and to keep him from playing up Long Hollow, where there was a still. Long Hollow was across Paddle Creek Road from the Pinkerman home.

David Blankenship, who was also raised on Paddle Creek, up Tar Camp Road, remembers when he was a child and played in an old cave further up the hollow than his house was. Inside the cave he found remnants of an old still. He also remembers where his Great-uncle Tom Kelly's still was, in Kimble Hollow, which is also off of Paddle Creek, but nearer to the Pinkerman residence. David told me his dad, Bill Blankenship, was somehow involved in moonshining, but was never arrested for it. Bill did not have his own still. Since Tom Kelly was a relative, it is likely that Dave's dad worked for or with him or for Jim Pinkerman, as Jim was said to have over seventy employees.

One of my Ironton High School classmates, Jim Volgares, told me about his grandfather, Fletcher Miller. Mr. Miller, the son of Andrew Jackson Miller and Magnolia Adkins Miller, was from Franklin Furnace and resided in Scioto County. "Fletch" served five years for moonshine-related charges while a resident of Ohio Furnace in Scioto County, yet was the only one of Andrew Jackson Miller's sons to not die a violent death. After serving his five-year illicit manufacturing sentence, he began employment as a dynamite blaster to prepare the excavation for the construction of the atomic energy plant in Piketon. From there he moved his family to Baltimore, Maryland, where he was employed as a steelworker and built ships during World War II. When the war ended, he moved back to southern Ohio and was a laborer at the Alpha Portland Cement Company. He later became an Ironton city employee at the sanitation department from which he retired. At one time he owned four homes in Ironton. "Fletch' raised his children without further incident or conflict with the law, was a devoted husband, loving father and grandfather. He died in 1978 at his home at 1414 South Second Street in Ironton.

Fletch's daughter, Gladys Miller Volgares, was teased as a child about her father having been a moonshiner. As an adult, she refused to talk to her children about anything to do with her father's imprisonment, even when they specifically asked.

Jim's great-grandfather, Andrew Jackson Miller, is not to be confused with Andrew Jackson (Jack) Miller, spouse of Helen Delawder Miller, as they were not of the same generation. However there is a great possibility the two may have been related, since both came to Ohio from Kentucky. There is no evidence readily available to verify the kinship.

Fletcher Miller in the 1960's

Ron Searls of Marion, Ohio, my son-in-law, has family connections with moonshiners too. His paternal grandfather, Noel Searls, was born and raised in New Straitsville and worked in the coal mines there. Ron recently told me about his maternal great-grandfather, Albert T. Riley, who was born in Kentucky, but moved to southern Ohio as a small child. Ron related a tragic story regarding the dangers of distilling, far more serious than evading revenuers and jail cells. During Prohibition and the Great Depression, Albert Riley worked as a laborer at a shoe factory in

Portsmouth, Scioto County, Ohio. He was young, married and the father of three small children. Sometime between the 1930 census and 1932 (the worst year of the Depression, according to www.hyperhistory.com's Timeline of the Great Depression) times got so tough the shoe factory was having difficulty staying profitable, so the administrators decided to lay off some of the factory's employees. Young Albert voluntarily took a layoff so one of his older co-workers with more children could stay on the job. Albert told his friend he would be able to support his small family by making moonshine. Thus, Albert set up a still and started manufacturing whisky. However, the distillation venture didn't last long. On November 4, 1932, Albert's still exploded and killed him before his thirtieth birthday, leaving a young widow and three small children behind during the worst years of the greatest depression in our country's history.

 Being of the tough, determined and hardworking character of our Appalachian culture, Riley's children survived and taught their offspring to be proud of their heritage. My dear granddaughter Kaitlyn (Searls), although never a resident of southern Ohio, is descended from Appalachian moonshiners via both her mother's and father's ancestors.

 Descendants of Thomas Jenkins, in Marion, Kitts Hill and Coal Grove, have told me he was in the business. He made and sold moonshine for several years. According to his daughter, Betty, Tom was never suspected, caught or arrested. By the time I knew him, he had quit distilling because the economy improved and he found gainful employment as a truck driver to provide for his family. Throughout his life he worked for the Markin Blanton Feed Company in Ironton, the Liquid Transporters in Ashland, Kentucky, and Lightning Fuel in Coal Grove, Ohio.

When I was a child, the Jenkins property bordered ours. Tom's children and grandchildren, the Massie boys, were my schoolmates and some have been my lifelong friends.

A few of us to this day stay in contact and communicate on a regular basis. Tom and Ruth, his wife, were good neighbors and their children and grandchildren were successful in school and have been successful in the community and in life. His youngest son, Benny, was in my class and looked much like Tom did in the photo of him as a young man.

When driving truck, Tom wore a chauffeur's cap and I don't remember ever seeing him without it.

Like my mother's family, Tom too was related to the Neals. However, we never considered the Jenkins family as our kin.

Thomas Jenkins as a young man

Tom Jenkins in his chauffeur's cap,
long after his moonshining days

Tom taught the techniques of the distillation trade to his sons and grandsons years before his death in 1988. Hopefully, they will pass the skills, techniques and recipes down through the generations in order to keep the custom alive within our culture.

When the Jenkins family ran out of product, they made purchases from the Yates family, the Delawder family, or the Fradd family.

Earl Fradd (1914-1987) reportedly made and sold moonshine in Lawrence County to help support his large family during the downward spiral of the U.S. economy, but never drank it. He had a large, active still so far up a hollow off of Oak Ridge Road and so high into those Lawrence County hills that no one ever found it. Because he didn't drink the stuff, he was never suspected, caught or arrested. Once the Depression was over, Earl found good

The above photo of Earl Fradd was taken many years after his manufacturing days.

employment and provided well for his family. He had a child in every grade with us Thorntons. His daughter Betty was in my class and she and I both currently reside in the same town, Marion, Ohio. Earl's wife was a Reynolds from Paddle Creek and her mother was a Rucker from Rucker Ridge. She was also related to the Delongs, which makes her distant kin to my mother. Like the Jenkins family, although distant kin, we Thornton children did not consider the Fradd family as our relatives.

Again, moonshining was a huge family business, especially when one considers the connections of the Delawder, Yates, Delong, Kelly, Fradd, Waugh, and Miller families. (Helen Delawder, daughter of Homer Delawder, married Andrew Jackson Miller.)

Robert Birchfield and Sadie Birchfield, his mother, lived in the last house up the hollow on New Castle Road beyond a coal tipple and mine once owned by Oakley Collins. Further up the hollow than their house they operated a small still of 18 to 20 gallons. Then on up the hollow in an old mine shaft was a larger still of 44-gallon capacity.

Ron Davis shared a story with me about his one purchase from the Birchfield still. It was 1957, and Ron was home on leave from the military. He and a buddy decided to buy a pint of spirits late one evening and while walking up the hollow to get it were attacked by the distillers' watchdog. Ron's friend shot the dog to prevent it from injuring him. Davis warned his friend not to let the Birchfields know about the dog incident or they may not want to sell them their product. Evidently, the Birchfields did not hear the shot and sold them the pint. The two young men made their getaway and the facts of the dog's death were never revealed to its owners.

Young Bob Birchfield was born in 1952 and has been an Elizabeth Township Trustee for seven terms. He related to me that his dad and grandmother did not go out to deliver or sell their moonshine. People came there to buy it. Eventually, Robert, Senior, and Sadie got caught and arrested. Robert served one year and one day in the state prison at Lucasville and Sadie served her time in Marysville, the only state facility for female offenders. The Lucasville prison, Southern Ohio Correctional Facility, was constructed in 1972, and I worked as a social worker there for over three years following its opening.

Although the Birchfields manufactured independently, they were aware of others in the area in the same business, including the Pinkermans and John and Minnie Scott. One of the Pinkermans shared with the Birchfields that Jim Pinkerman regularly delivered as far away as North Carolina, but left that job when he obtained a position as driver for Waylon Jennings. Pinkerman stayed with the Jennings driving job until he died.

Young Bob is proud of his dad and grandmother. He realizes they worked hard to make a living during difficult times with the few resources available to them.

According to the information obtained through my research, the Birchfields were the most recent moonshiners arrested and sentenced from Lawrence County.

It seems the one-year-and-a day sentence was popular with judges back in the day. My Uncle Marion also got sentenced for one year and a day, as did some others mentioned previously, according to old newspaper articles.

In the spring of 2011, while attending a book signing in the library of Rock Hill High School, Anita Sanders Scherer, a school office worker, shared a humorous story with Sharon Sites Eaches, Ron Thomas, Dennis Hankins (Rock Hill School Board President) and me about two local preachers, Charles Jayne and Dennis Hankins. The preachers came to her home many years ago to visit her now-deceased husband, Bill Roberts, and to encourage him to return to regular church attendance. Bill invited the two men of God into his kitchen to sit around the table to chat with him. Inside his kitchen, much to their surprise, a small moonshine still was actively working on the kitchen stove and dripping spirits into a container near the sink.

Dennis Hankins in 2011

Dennis, a terrific fellow who has lived a blessed life for God, country and community, confirmed her story and explained preachers in the hills were apt to run into some unique situations. He continued with a story of when as a child being raised by his grandparents he remembered his grandfather made some secretive alcoholic beverages in the cellar and the men went in there while the women overlooked their actions. We all had a good laugh.

Bill Roberts (John William Roberts) was voted as the guy with the best personality in his 1961 graduating class at Rock Hill High School. Although he distilled for medicinal purposes, he was not a man anyone, especially the two preachers, would ever suspect of having a moonshine still.

Anita continued entertaining us by telling about a previous still gone sour at the home of Bill's mother, Ruth Roberts. Ruth did not approve of stills and ordered her son to dispose of the soured mash. She also fussed about the stench, which was so disgustingly pungent Bill had to put a clothespin on his nose to be able to breathe to carry the mash to the nearest creek to dump it.

Bill, one of my generation, continued making moonshine, beer and wine for his own use a while longer. He learned the process from his mother-in-law, a relative of Jim Pinkerman. Well-liked by all who knew him and respected in his community, Bill died in 1983 at the age of thirty-nine. He is greatly missed by his family and friends.

Bill Roberts in 1979

Butch Massie, Tom Jenkins's grandson, told me his now-deceased stepfather, Carl Lloyd Smith, who we all called "Smitty", distilled moonshine in a shed on the family property, which was a fifteen-acre plot known as the old Kessinger place. (Smitty purchased the land from his friend, my brother Ronnie.) Somewhere on this property near a large orchard, he buried numerous gallons of his spirits for aging and to prevent it from being seen by anyone outside the immediate family. Carl did not tell anyone of the precise location and enjoyed taunting his eleven stepsons with the suspense of the secrecy. Although he had been ill, Smitty died unexpectedly in 1988 at the age of 55, and no one in the family has ever been able to locate his hidden treasure.

Carl Lloyd Smith (Smitty)

Smitty manufactured well into my lifetime and also into my children's, but was never suspected or caught. Until his illness, he worked as a machinist for Wayne Pump, National Mines and the General Machine Shop in Ironton.

The Sprouse brothers, Proctor, Bill and Don were active manufacturers into the 1950's. According to Ted Sprouse, his Uncle Proctor got caught twice and once was because of his kindness. Proctor's brothers tried to warn him about folks in their line of business taking in strangers, but

Proctor was determined to help out someone a little worse off than he. He let a guy stay with him for a couple of weeks, believing he needed a roof over his head. Proctor kindly provided the roof. However, the man didn't share an important fact with Sprouse; he worked for the IRS. Although the situation seemed to be entrapment, Proctor was arrested by the very man he was giving a home, charged and sent to prison. Bill and Don never did any time.

Don's young son, Ted, wanted to learn the family business, but Don wanted a better life for him and wouldn't teach him, so his Uncle Bill did. Don did not want his son to ever be arrested or to have to do time.

Ted didn't want to learn the process to get into the family business as a lifelong career. He respected his father and uncles and realized they did what they had to do to survive the tough economic times and to support themselves and their families. They couldn't find a decent-paying job, so like all the others mentioned previously, created their own by manufacturing and selling whisky. The reason Ted wanted to learn the process was to carry on and preserve a part of his Appalachian culture. Uncle Bill not only taught Ted the process, but taught others in the younger generation as well.

Finally, after many years of teaching and distilling, Ted's Uncle Bill was caught and arrested when Bill Sprouse was nearly eighty years of age. Old Sprouse was threatened with prison time and given a choice; if he didn't make any more moonshine, they'd let him go free. Bill wouldn't agree to the condition. Nor would he lie. He was an honest man. He told the judge he didn't get much Social Security to live on and refused to accept any welfare as long as he could earn his own living and at his age making moonshine was the only way he knew how to do it. (By this time the old copper still had worn out and Bill was using the thumper as a smaller-sized still.) The judge was evidently impressed with the old man's determination to make it on his own and dismissed his case.

Ted didn't know the name of the revenuer who arrested his uncles either time, but advised me a man by the name of Bill Stapleton was somehow involved.

John and Minnie Scott lived on a farm at Dog Fork, Kitts Hill, until the early 1950's. They kept the farm property, but moved to a new home on Crow Ridge. Their still was found long after they had moved from Dog Fork. Although no one was living on the farm property at the time (1956), they were charged for having a still and for possession of moonshine. They received only probation, as they had not actually produced any spirits for approximately six years. However, they did have in their possession some moonshine from when the still in their farm's smokehouse was active.

According to their son George the Lawrence County Sheriff at the time was Carl Rose and the deputy who investigated was John Drake. The Scott's 250 gallon capacity copper pot still was confiscated by Deputy Drake and used for displays at fairs and festivals in the area for several years.

George Scott and my brother Ronnie went through all twelve grades of school together and graduated in 1960 from Rock Hill High School. George's older brother Vernon Elwood was valedictorian of the Rock Hill High School Class of 1955, and another older brother John played football for Ohio State. After serving in the U.S. Marine Corps, he was contacted by the American Football

League and was selected to play professional football. In the early 1960's, John played for the Buffalo Bills.

Minnie Scott in 1962

At one time Minnie worked for a flower shop in Ironton. She used the knowledge and experience from this job to open her own business, Scott's Flower Shop, at Fourth and

Vernon Streets in Ironton. John, Senior, was employed by Armco Steel. Their sons currently own and operate a multi-million dollar business (according to manta.com/c/mm29673/scott-chemical-co) at 1220 South Third Street in Ironton, Scotts Chemical Company.

The Scotts were good citizens, provided well for their family, and were respected by others in the community. John Scott died in 1980. Minnie died in 2005.

Neither the Marvin J. Siders mentioned in the indictment as a co-conspirator, nor his offspring, could be located for an interview. However, Mavis Siders Ratliff, daughter of Lee (Leland Siders) was contacted. Mavis, a 1947 graduate of Rock Hill High School, currently resides in Florida and has not lived in Ohio for many years. She explained her father had spent time in a penal facility in Wilmington, Ohio, for moonshining. She has a cousin named Marvin Beauford Siders who is around eighty, is retired from the Air Force and now lives in Raleigh, North Carolina. His dad was called "Puss" Siders and he also was a moonshiner, along with his brother, Lee. Mavis was raised by her grandparents, John and Frances Siders, who lived on a dirt road off Oak Ridge Road, but she doesn't remember its name. There is a Beauford Siders listed in the 1930 Census as a son of John, and brother to Leland, but no Marvin or Marvin J. (Mavis's husband Carl was a co-worker and dear friend of my deceased brother Ronnie and is still a friend of David Blankenship.)

Mavis related a story about a man coming to visit her home when she was a small child. The visitor asked Mavis if her daddy (Lee) was home, because he was not at the house when the fellow arrived. Mavis told the man he was home, but working back on the hill. She took him to her father, who was busy tending his still. When the visitor left,

Lee explained to Mavis that she was to not ever take anyone else to the still again, as a visitor could be a revenuer instead of a friend.

As with the Fradd, Jenkins and Waugh families, there was a Blankenship in the class of each of the five Thornton children. Some of Tom Jenkins' grandchildren were also in classes with some of my siblings and me. However, I can only recall one Siders child in school with us, Jimmy Siders, and he was in my younger brother Bill's class.

Lyndall Murdock Eubanks, another of my Ironton High School classmates and a former teacher with the Dawson Bryant School District in Coal Grove, shared information about her father, a successful businessman and convicted moonshiner, Lowell Murdock.

Lowell was born September 27, 1914. At twenty-one he married a young bride of only fourteen years of age. During the economic crises of the 1930's, Lowell and his father-in-law, Gerard Locey, were having difficulty making it financially on the family's farm in Proctorville. Lowell did not drink, but decided he could supplement the family income by manufacturing and selling whisky. In 1936 he was caught and arrested at their still, but Gerard got away and was not charged. Lowell had to leave his wife and baby, Vivian, to serve six months and one day at the federal correctional facility in Chillicothe.

Like many of the other manufacturers in this chapter, when released from prison, Lowell was never in any kind of trouble again. He was owner and operator of Murdock Used Cars in Ironton for thirty-seven years and, in addition to his dealership, also worked at Armco Steel and the Dayton Malleable Iron Company. Although he had other real estate, he owned and resided for fifty-seven years at 420 Oak Street in Ironton. He raised four children: Vivian, Donna, Lowell and Lyndall.

Lowell Murdock, Senior, was a devoted husband, married to the same wife for seventy-two years at the time of his death (September 30, 2007) at age ninety-three. He was also a loving father and excellent provider for his family. In addition to his accomplishments and the achievements of his children, all of his six grandchildren, now adults, are college graduates and are proudly following in the successful footsteps of their grandfather Murdock.

As you've probably figured by now, making moonshine has been a part of southern Ohio's, Lawrence County's and my family's Appalachian culture for generations.
Numerous people were involved. Like many of the other distinct cultural traits, the distillation process is passed from one generation to the next through hands-on experience. Not all of our people are or were moonshiners. Some were into law enforcement, farming and other careers. Some were and are educated professionals. Unlike the stereotype of a toothless fellow lying around with his head on a log and a crock jug of whisky in his hand, wearing a straw hat and bib overalls with no shirt, and a few teeth missing, these men were considered to be honest, hardworking, industrious fellows earning a living to support their families while providing a service to their communities. They were not looked down on by family members or by their neighbors. Many were churchgoing folks who were appreciated and respected for being ambitious enough to find a way to support themselves and for surviving the difficult national economy.

Like the families in the movie *Thunder Road,* repectable folks in southern Ohio made moonshine, but attended church. They didn't consider it immoral or criminal, as it was the way they survived. However unlike the movie, in southern Ohio few folks were shot to death by federal agents and there were not bullies who tried to control all of the stills and the revenue from them.

Not everyone can get a liquor license. Few can get a permit to distill and manufacture spirits for beverages, even if they follow the lengthy application process, pay all the taxes and do all the required government reports in a timely fashion.

There's an old saying, "When things get tough, the tough get going." The people described in this book were living during tough times and they did what they had to do to keep on going. I don't think the people who make moonshine now or the ones who made it in the past do/did it to conspire against the government or because they choose/chose a life of crime or to cheat on their taxes. They make spirits, wine and beer now for their own use and because it is a part of their heritage. Those of the past made liquor not only as a part of their culture, but also as a means of survival when jobs were scarce and the economy made farming unreliable as a means of income.

In the next chapter, you will learn of some of the methods, techniques and recipes used by the distillers in the Appalachian area of southern Ohio and other places within the Appalachian region.

Chapter 10

Culture, Cooks and Chemistry

There are many tricks of the moonshine distillation trade and not everyone is willing to give up their secrets. There are recipes on the internet, in family cookbooks, and in numerous other books and blogs. Ingredients can also vary. Some folks use corn, keep it in a barrel for a few days and let it sprout for mash, then add the yeast. Others prefer rye to corn. Some use malt.

Moonshining is such an important part of our Appalachian culture that in 1963-64, when I was a junior, we made and drank it and the mash in our chemistry lab at Ironton High School. Miss Loraine C. Tufts was our teacher, a pleasant woman and Justice of the Peace from Kentucky noted for her mischievous smile. Although she was old and approaching the age of retirement, she was well-liked by her students. There is a photograph in our senior yearbook of one of her labs with the caption, "Tuffy's Tavern".

Recently, I asked a few classmates if any of them remembered how we made it back then. Only Don Thacker did and this is his response in an e-mail to me dated February 23, 2011:

> "I remember the main ingredient as being Karo syrup, light or dark. I believe Karo now has some salt added so the salt may prevent it from fermenting. In order to ferment, you would need some basic bread yeast that is dissolved in a cup of warm water (not hot) before adding this

to the syrup. There needs to be some extra water added, but not sure how much. Once added, I think that it needs to sit at room temperature until it starts to bubble.

Also, once it starts cooking/boiling, it needs to pass thru coils of copper that are surrounded by ice so that it can re-liquify. Re-boiling this initial liquid is what increases the alcohol content.

I think that this might get you started. If jailbirds can make hooch from orange juice and old bread, this could work."

My memories of drinking the mash and moonshine are more vivid than the laboratory process. After all, it was about forty-seven years ago. Another classmate, Paula Penotte Kitts, now a resident of Marion, Ohio, and I were recently discussing how we carried our test tubes of spirits around the school with us so we could take a swig when desired. Chemistry was a fun class and a good cultural education experience. We used Bunsen burners in the lab as the heat source for the distillation process and never questioned any school or law enforcement authorities about the legalities because we were too busy enjoying the final product.

In the 1970's I worked as a social worker at Southern Ohio Correctional Facility in Lucasville and certainly became familiar with "hooch" production. The inmates, or residents, as they preferred being called, took fruit and bread from the cafeteria to their cells for snacks. They squeezed juice from oranges, apples and other fruit into containers and put the bread into the liquid for a yeast source. The inmates who worked in the cafeteria sometimes got sugar for them to help in the fermentation process and the "hooch" was shared with cell mates.

In the Ironton Memorial Day Parade, the longest continuing Memorial Day Parade in the United States, each year there are reminders of our moonshine heritage along with the flags and floats honoring our veteran heroes. The New Straitsville Moonshine Festival is always during the Memorial Day weekend and also celebrates with a parade on Memorial Day. There are plenty of stills displayed along both parades with hill folks dressed in bib overalls, black felt hats, straw hats, and barefoot with ceramic jugs for a cool swig in the hot weather. Outhouses are pulled on trucks and wagons and are decorated for the occasion. There is usually a float or two with some good ole country pickin' and singin'. It's all a part of the cultural celebration.

The above photo was taken at the Ironton Memorial Day Parade, May 30, 2011.

Backside view of the previous photo

Moonshine Express, a remotely controlled miniature vehicle, in the Ironton Memorial Day Parade, 2011

During a telephone conversation a few days before the 2011 Memorial Day weekend, Ted Sprouse discussed his family's distillation business and how his uncles once used syrupy canned fruit instead of sugar in their moonshine. They also dried peaches in the oven to color their spirits instead of using the charred barrels my family did. Others have told me they have used overly ripe fruit and much less sugar.

Smitty's family sometimes added fresh pears for flavor, as his still was near an orchard.

Uncle Forrest used only distilled water in his manufacturing process and blended his whisky to make it no less than 100 proof. The Sprouses used the numbered drip containers to lessen the proof. According to *Our Journey Continues,* the folks in New Straitsville used sulphur water in their process, believing it gave their product a distinct taste. They also believed using the mine's shaft to hide the stills and to maintain the process at a steady underground temperature (approximately 56 degrees F) improved the quality of their product. They used a hydrometer to measure the proof instead of the bubbles or "frogs' eyes" that my uncles and the Sprouse brothers used. The Sprouses preferred keeping their product between 80 and 100 proof. The New Straitsville group put charred wood chips inside the whisky for color and used funnels and black felt hats to strain/filter it before placing the moonshine in corked ceramic jugs or jars. "Rot gut" is what they called the product of the guys who put oil in their moonshine to get it to bead.

My uncles, and others in Lawrence County, charred the inside of oak wood kegs and stored the moonshine in them for up to a year to age and to give it the desired golden brown color.

While at the 2011 Moonshine Festival in Perry County, Ohio, I took a photo of a sign hanging in the booth with the active still. The sign had some history of the village from the 1930's. It said, "of 42 stills taken into Perry County Court, 37 were from New Straitsville". That doesn't sound all so impressive, unless one knows a little more about the place. According to the 2000 census, the village covers an area of 1.3 square miles and contains only 774 people in 312 households. When considering its size, 37 stills that were confiscated coming from 312 homes means more than ten percent of the households were caught moonshining. There were plenty who did not get caught because they tended to build their stills inside the deserted coal mines. Those in the town who didn't make it bought and sold the grain, sugar, yeast, jars, charcoal and other materials needed or used their storefronts and businesses as distribution centers. The children were the lookouts for the revenuers and had well-planned, yet discreet ways of warning the moonshiners when a stranger arrived in their village. The women washed and sterilized the jugs. (Several of the homes had secret storage compartments to hide the product.) Folks who had cars delivered it to Columbus, Chicago and New York. The townsfolk claim nearly everyone was involved in the distillation business in one way or another, even the town's priest. The community encapsulated the distillers, because conversely, subsequent to the burning of the coal mines, moonshining was the economic livelihood of the people.

According to New Straitsville folks, the first step in the distillation process was making or setting the mash, a mixture of cane sugar, cracked corn, rye grain, yeast and water. It took a barrel about eight days to ferment to ten to twelve percent alcohol. After fermenting, the wash, the liquid part of the mash that contained the alcohol, was taken out, strained and put into the still, which was heated by gas or kerosene burners because the steady heat they provided produced little smoke. (Other fuels were also used, including wood and coal, but not as frequently.) When the wash reached the point of distillation, steam traveled up through the coiled copper tubing, or the worm, and to the cooling barrel where it ran down through the drip tube into the ceramic jug, or glass gallon jar. Some moonshiners distilled the whisky a second time to obtain a higher proof.

I took a photo of the license the festival committee obtains and displays in order to exhibit a working still and noted it is an "ALCOHOL FUEL PRODUCERS PERMIT UNDER 26 U.S.C. 5181" and is specified "not for consumption." The framed permit, dated 2001, was hung inside the building with the working still and was visible to onlookers. Viewers could not touch the still or walk around it due to safety issues.

Active still at the New Straitsville
Moonshine Festival 2011

Malissa, Fred Hawk and Michal enjoying the midway at the 1989 Moonshine Festival

Smitty and the Jenkins family measured their yeast, sugar and corn, put them into barrels along with some water and let the mixture process (or work) for 10-14 days. Large light bulbs were placed near the barrels for warmth to speed up the process. Once the mixture had properly fermented, they put it into a copper kettle with a collector on the top. A copper coil went out of the top and when the ingredients were boiling, the steam condensed and from that a drip in a steady stream of unusable liquid formed. The first gallon was too strong, or too high in alcohol content, so was used to blend other jugs of drip to the desired taste and alcohol proof. When the mixture first started condensing, it was milky and could not be used. Once it became clear, it was caught in a jug, jar or bucket. If and when the drip became milky again, it was not used for drink or mix, not even an ounce. The rest of the drip was blended with the first. Once all of the clear drip was caught, the mash was fed to the hogs. It made them happy and fattened them up for pork chops, hams and bacon.

Cooks.com describes the making of white lightning in steps. The first is to convert the starch of the grain into sugar (professional distillers use malt). The shelled whole corn is put into a container and covered in warm water. There is supposed to be a hole in the bottom of the container and a hot cloth is to be placed over it. As the warm water drains off, more is to be put in to replace it for up to three days, or until the corn has sprouts of about two inches. The corn is then dried and ground into meal. The meal is mixed with boiling water into a mush or mash. Rye mash can be mixed the same way and added at this time, but is not necessary.

Yeast is mixed in the amount of one-half pound to each fifty gallons of mash to speed up the fermentation. If yeast is not used, the fermentation process will last ten or more days instead of about four. The mixture must be kept warm to ferment.

When the mash stops working (or bubbling up) and settles down, it is ready to run. During this stage, the mash converts into carbonic acid and alcohol. It is sour to taste and is called beer or wash.

The cooker, or still, has two main parts, a top and bottom. The mash is put into the bottom, a copper tub, and the top is pasted on with dough or some other paste. If the pressure from the heat of the fire builds up, the dough will give way and prevent an explosion.

In the top of the cooker is a copper pipe sometimes called an arm. It goes to one side and tapers down to the diameter of the worm, usually about one inch to one and one-fourth of an inch. Dough is also put at any other connection in the pipes.

The cooks.com process described bending the coil with the ends stopped up and filled with sand to prevent the pipe from kinking. The coil, or worm, is then cleaned and attached firmly to the end of the arm and placed inside a barrel full of cold, running water that runs from the top and out an opening in the bottom so it can circulate better.

Under the cooker a fire is lit that causes the spirit to rise in a vapor with the steam. It goes into the arm, then through the coil into the cold water to condense. The condensation is collected at the end of the coil into a container.

This article described the first run-off, or "singlings", as weak and impure and further states it must be redistilled to rid it of rank oils and water.

The second run-off, called "doublings", is put into the cleaned cooker along with the "singlings" and some water; then it gets heated so it can run through the coil again.

The first quart out is far too strong for use (about 200 proof) and the last drippings will be only about 10 proof, or too weak. The skill is in making the mix into 100 proof.

As per cooker.com:

"If a tablespoon of the liquid does not 'flash' or burn when thrown on the fire, there is not enough alcohol left to bother running any more."

It is suggested to use a small glass vial to test for proof. Small bubbles will rise if the vial is slanted. When the bubbles (frogs' eyes) are half above and half below the top of the liquid, then it is the correct proof. After the bubble test, the product is filtered by running it through charcoal. Once this is done, the liquid is ready to be consumed.

The cooks.com recipe does not indicate how many gallons of moonshine are produced from the ingredients via the fifty gallons of mash. Nor does it advise how much sugar, corn or water to use. Without the amounts, it isn't of much use as a recipe.

I found a blog online at www.absoluteastronomy.com/discussionpost that answers questions about making moonshine. The blog could be very helpful, but one should be careful about what he or she writes. Web sites are used to trap sex offenders and that is a good thing, because they are dangerous criminals. However, the web could also be used by federal officers to entrap moonshiners since users can be traced. One might be better off to order one of the many books on how to make the stuff from amazon.com. You'd think the ATF would be more concerned about terrorists or meth labs, but we all know how important the almighty dollar can be to Uncle Sam and the IRS, so be careful about using blogs and making purchases with your credit card or checks.

The following drawing is a little more helpful because the amounts of ingredients are given. The amounts were suggested in the New Straitsville Local History Group's *Our Journey Continues*.

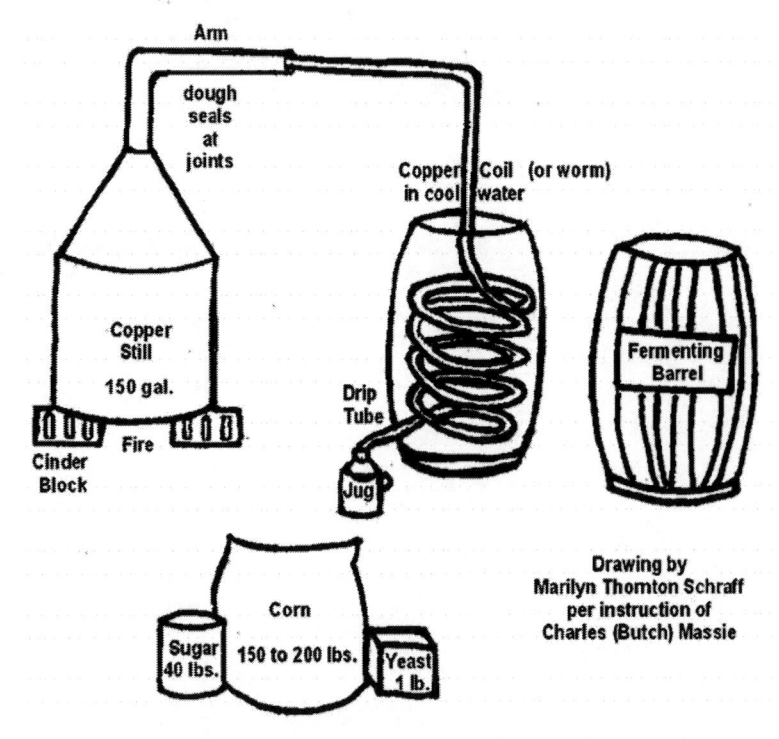

Diagram labels: Arm; dough seals at joints; Copper Coil (or worm) in cool water; Copper Still 150 gal.; Drip Tube; Fire; Cinder Block; Jug; Fermenting Barrel; Sugar 40 lbs.; Corn 150 to 200 lbs.; Yeast 1 lb.

Drawing by Marilyn Thornton Schraff per instruction of Charles (Butch) Massie

Above is a drawing of an alcohol-for-consumption still without a thumper.

It is important to keep the distiller and all equipment and containers clean and sterile. Once distilled and bottled, it is recommended the spirits be stored at underground temperature (approximately 56 degrees Fahrenheit), like in a cellar or basement. My family used a trench so the tops of the jugs would be approximately two feet below ground level. The jugs were then covered with leaves for easy access and to be hidden in a natural environment from the revenuers. The New Straitsville folks kept theirs in underground coal mines. Smitty buried his.

There are numerous resources online for building various types of homemade distilleries. Many include diagrams and/or photographs. The Blue Ridge Institute describes three basic types of stills: the turnip (shown in the drawing on the previous page), the blackpot (or blackpot submarine) and the steam still.

In the copper turnip still a foam, called the cap, forms during fermentation. The warmer the weather, the fewer days it takes to ferment. When the cap goes away, the remaining mixture is between 6% to 12% alcohol and is called beer, which is put into the turnip-shaped pot to be distilled by fire. The mixture must be stirred so it won't scorch and puke into the worm. It should be kept consistently at alcohol's boiling point of 173 degrees Fahrenheit. The cap is secured and the steam goes through the coil to cool, then drips the whisky into a jar, jug or bucket.

The blackpot still is usually made from boards and sheets of galvanized steel, but can be copper, and can hold far more gallons of mash than the turnip still. With this larger still, the mash is mixed directly in the boiler. To make 800 gallons, according to the Blue Ridge website, one would need about:

> "50 pounds of rye meal, 50 pounds of barley meal, 800 pounds of sugar and water. Two 80-pound sacks of wheat bran are poured on top of the mixture to hold in the heat of fermentation."

Once the mixture has fermented, the mixture is heated and stirred. When the mash is near the desired distillation temperature, the cap is fastened on top of the boiler. The vapors travel into a doubler, or thumper, that has been filled with mash beer or a weaker whisky. The vapors from the heat in the boiler heat the beer/whisky mix in the doubler, making the alcohol originally contained in the still go though a second distillation while saving the time and labor of running the singlings through the still again. This also serves to smooth the taste of the moonshine. The condensation then goes from the doubler into the water-cooled worm and flows out as a liquid. According to the "Institute", well-cleaned car radiators have been used as condensers instead of the coiled worm. After the blackpot still has been run once, the distillers add more sugar and start the process again, up to six or seven runs to get the limit of acceptable whisky from one batch of mash. The blackpot method produces larger amounts of lower quality spirits.

The Blue Ridge recipe further explains that, "The sugar added to the mash recipe hastens the fermentation and produces a higher alcohol content." This makes more whisky for the same amount of effort, or a higher output.

A steam still is defined by answers.com/topic/steam-still as:

> "a still in which steam provides most of the heat; distillation requires a lower

temperature than in standard equipment, except for a vacuum distillation unit".

The steam still is not as common as the others and has several designs, but they work basically the same. A boiler containing water is heated to the desired temperature and the steam is released into the fermented mash or is piped to the mash container. The mash boils and the vapors or spirits pass into a water-cooled thumper or into a coiled worm. The advantages of using the steam method are that the mash doesn't scorch or doesn't have to be stirred and the still works faster than the other types.

There are plenty of good ideas out there for using some modern conveniences in the distillation process. For example, it was stated on the blog mentioned earlier in this chapter that electric coils like those used to heat water in household water heaters can be used for the heat source in distilling (rather than open flames) and that they are easily obtainable for a reasonable price. An engineer told me a simple pressure valve could be put on the cook pot of a still, which would eliminate the need for a thumper or dough use for seals. The pressure valve, like the dough, would also prevent explosions. I found a photo of one online at homedistiller.org/image/mini-explained.jpg that looked like the valve on a pressure cooker. Some distillers have told me they use Coleman coolers filled with ice to cool the copper coils instead of running water.

A great photo of a mini-still with drawings and nineteen pages of detailed verbal explanation on how to set it up can be found online at: homedistiller.org/image/mini_ explained.jpg.

A moonshine recipe from http: www.blueridge institute.org/moonshine/1980's_mash_recipe_for_corn_ liquor.html reads as follows:

"These ingredients are for one 55-gallon mash barrel. (Most moonshiners use a 48" X 32" wooden mash box, and recipe amounts are adjusted accordingly.)

50 lbs. of plain white cornmeal. (The meal should not be self-rising, and it should be ground slowly at the mill so the meal does not get too hot)

25 lbs. of rye meal

12.5 lbs of ground barley malt

25 lbs. of sugar (The sugar is only used if the weather is too hot.)

2 packages of yeast

Heat 18 gallons of water to 172 degrees and pour into the barrel. Add the corn meal to the water and mix until fine - no lumps. Add the rye meal and mix until fine. Let mixture sit for 1.5 hours. Transfer a few gallons of the mixture into a separate bucket and stir in 11 lbs. of malt. Mix well and pour back into the barrel. Again mix well.

Sprinkle 1.5 lbs of malt on the top surface of the barrel mixture and let sit for 45 minutes. When the malt on the surface cracks, begin stirring the mash, working gradually to the bottom of the barrel. Stir until the temperature of the mash drops to the point you can stir with your bare hand. Fill the remainder of the barrel with water, keeping the mash between 84 and 90 degrees. (If the weather is too hot, add the sugar to keep the mash temperature in the proper range.)

Put a small amount of mash in a separate bucket and mix in two packages of yeast. When the mixture begins foaming up, pour it back into the mash barrel. Stir well and cover, but not tightly. In about three hours the entire barrel will be fermenting. In about three days the mash will be ready to distill."

The Blue Ridge 1980's recipe is one of few that states the amounts of water to be added. It is similar to the recipe used by the Jenkins and Smith families at Kitts Hill, Ohio, because it uses white corn meal instead of whole or cracked corn. If the yeast is not added, it takes the mixture 10-14 days to ferment instead of three days.

The Sprouse brothers used white whole corn and cracked corn, yeast, sugar, warm water for it to work or ferment in, a two-burner gas hot plate, a 55-gallon copper barrel, and a barrel of cold water to cool the coil. They used a thumper, a gadget that is attached to the arm pipe to go to a little tank through the barrel to the coil. They preferred using numbered glass jugs to catch the drip because it made blending according to proof easier. If the still boiled over into the thumper tank, or puked, it could ruin the whisky.

Bill Sprouse wouldn't use a thumper. He believed in tending to the distillation process attentively so that a thumper wouldn't be needed. He used dough to seal joint seams. As the dough was heated by the steam in the pipes, it baked and formed a hard seal. Yet, under pressure, the baked dough would come off and let out enough steam to prevent an explosion. Over-heating was avoided because losing steam meant losing alcohol.

Uncle Bill taught Ted how to blend their product and to cut it down with only whisky. No water was used. The first gallon to drip was over 200 proof and would take the skin off a tongue. Five to six gallons of whisky were produced from a 55-gallon drum of mash. It was as clear as water. The remainder of the mash was fed to the hogs.

The second jug to the fifth or sixth jug had a bit of a blue to green tint to it. It was used instead of water for blending to the desired 80 proof.

The beads at the top of the product, or frogs' eyes, were used to determine proof. The larger the beads, the higher the proof, with 1/32 of an inch being the desired size. The smaller beads were formed in spirits of a lower proof. Bill stirred the mixture with a dipper to get bubbles, or beads, the size he wanted in the jugs.

According to Ted, when moonshine is burned, a blue flame indicates good alcohol. One must hold a spoon of it in good light because it is difficult to see the color. If the flame is white, the whisky is not of a pure quality.

Bill Sprouse used charred oak barrels for color and aging, but learned he could get the same color in a shorter amount of time by baking peaches and dropping the dried chunks into the liquor. Once the desired color was obtained, the peach chunks were removed. The dried peach method shortened the processing time and helped increase profits.

Bill gladly taught his nephews and others how to distill and blend whisky because he wanted cultural traditions kept alive so each generation could pass them on to the next.

When government officials were closely watching grocery stores, the Sprouse brothers used caution. They devised a plan that depended on the many different members of the Sprouse family. Each of the wives, sisters and married nieces bought the yeast in small amounts. The married females in the family all had different last names and shopped at various grocery stores to make it more difficult for the enforcers to trace purchases to any one suspect.

According to family folklore, there was a train wreck near the Sprouse residence with Del Monte canned goods aboard as cargo. Uncle Bill gathered up all of the derailed cans of the syrupy fruit he could find, including numerous containers of fruit cocktail, peaches and pears. He used his newly found resource to increase his moonshine profits by using the sweet, syrupy fruit in lieu of sugar as an ingredient. Ted remembers hearing his uncle laughing as he proudly offered samples of his fruit cocktail and pear moonshine for taste comparisons.

Old Bill would be pleased with my research, as I accidentally learned that one of his nephews married into another moonshine family. However, the gal had no knowledge her father, Willard Waugh, was involved in the business because (according to George and Gene Waugh) Willard did not discuss it with any of his children.

It would be interesting to find some of Bill Sprouse's notes just to learn about how many people he taught to manufacture whisky during his lifetime. Hopefully those he did teach will pass along the traditions to their children, grandchildren, nieces and nephews.

The above photo is of a confiscated copper still on display at the 2011 Moonshine Festival.

The New Straitsville, Perry County, Ohio, Moonshine Festival was started in 1970 as part of the town's centennial celebration and continues today. The festival celebrates our Appalachian culture through New Straitsville's history of coal mining, unions and moonshine production. The cooks, chemists and distillers there and throughout southeastern Ohio have been a part of American and Ohio culture for hundreds of years.

Although New Straitsville claims to be the moonshine capital of the world, both Cosby, Tennessee, and Franklin County, Virginia, also call themselves the Moonshine Capital of the World. There are also Moonshine Festivals in Dawsonville, Georgia; Madison, North Carolina; and Campobello, South Carolina. The moonshine festivals in Dawsonville, Georgia, and Campobello, South Carolina, both started in 1967. The festival in Madison, North Carolina, began in 2009. Bluegrass festivals in many states have moonshine included in their celebrations, as far north as Columbus, Ohio. There is information available about an Annual Moonshiners Reunion held at Plum Hollow, Campobello, South Carolina, online at www.moonshiners.com/uploads/reunion.asp. One cannot doubt the impact moonshine has had and continues to have on our Appalachian culture.

The use of high school chemistry labs for distillation is legal with prior approval; but distillation of anything other than fuel alcohol is illegal anywhere in the U.S., basically because of the whisky tax revenue. It's ok to make limited amounts of beer and wine for one's own use, but not whisky. So if you plan to keep this part of our culture alive and celebrate it in the privacy of your own home, beware of blogs, snitches, Uncle Sam and the IRS.

Chapter 11

Remedies and Recipes

A couple of my favorite moonshine (or legal whisky) recipes are for a home remedy called a hot toddy and a mixed drink called apple pie. A recipe was found at http://www.ehow.com/how_4703180_hot-toddy-recipe.html quite similar to the one my grandmother (Mary Dilley) Thornton made for us when we sounded hoarse to her or coughed repeatedly. The instructions are as follows:

"Things you'll need: whisky, one lemon, one tablespoon of honey and hot water.

1. Gather all of the supplies needed to follow the hot-toddy recipe.
2. Decide which alcohol you want to use. You can either use whiskey, bourbon, rum or scotch. Depending on where you live, different areas have different traditions for which alcohol is best for use.
3. Boil a cup of water and set it aside. Mix your one shot (1 oz.) of alcohol of choice with a tablespoon of honey. Cut a slice of lemon to put into your hot toddy and squeeze the juice of the rest of the lemon into the mixture.
4. Pour your hot water over the mixture and stir until the honey is fully dis-

solved. Drink and enjoy. You will feel better in no time."

Modern day moms and grandmothers can heat the water in the microwave to save time.

The apple pie drink mixture used at our family get-togethers is as follows:

    1 pt. of moonshine (can be legal whisky or Everclear)
    ½ gal of apple juice
    ½ gal of apple cider
    3 sticks of cinnamon
    1 cup of sugar or Splenda (white or brown)

Mix all of the ingredients, except the alcohol, together and heat in a pan on the stove stirring to prevent the sugar from sticking to the pan and boil for approximately five minutes. Let the mixture cool for about ½ hour, add the moonshine (legal whisky or Everclear) and refrigerate until good and cool, preferably overnight.

Apple pie drink recipes similar to the one my family uses can be found at: http://www.drinknation. com/drink/apple_pie-bulk or at ehow.com.

As mentioned in Chapter 10, some moonshiners, including Bill Sprouse and Smitty, put various types of fruit in their spirits either to add color or flavor. According to the Blue Ridge Institute, "fruit liquor" was and continues to be popular. The Institute's website describes the process as loosely filling a half-gallon jar with fresh fruit, adding a cup of sugar, then filling with moonshine. The fruit liquor is then allowed to sit for a few weeks for the flavors to blend. After the few weeks the fruit mix could be used as is, or as a base for medicines.

I am familiar with folks using fruit, sugar or honey and boiling it in water to form a syrup. Once the syrup cools, moonshine and various herbs are added to form multiple mixed drinks or home remedies. For example, adding the mixture to a cup of hot sassafras tea with a shot (one ounce) of moonshine is said to be good for the digestive system, stomach aches, constipation, and similar ailments. Using onion instead of fruit to form the syrup, then adding peppermint leaves, eucalyptus greens or oil, or horehound candy to the cup of hot water and the shot of spirits is said to be good for cold and flu symptoms. Cherries or apples and cinnamon are commonly used in cough syrup.

Dad was big on the use of horehound candy being held in one's mouth as a cough suppressant or to loosen phlegm in the throat. He regularly kept a pan of water on the heating stove to put moisture into the air. When any of us got a cold or nasal stuffiness, he added eucalyptus leaves or oil to the water and the vapors helped clear the nasal passages. He also made us special teas to treat our ailments.

I have heard of parents giving ailing little folks liquor and honey or molasses on a homemade pacifier or putting it in a bottle of cow's milk with a rubber nipple to aid in restful sleep, but my mom was against giving hard liquor to an infant. I have also heard of folks rubbing liquor on the gums of a child who was cutting teeth. Sometimes an adult held a shot of whisky in his mouth awhile before swallowing it to help relieve the pain of a toothache.

In some of the old TV westerns, men were given whisky before an arrow or bullet was removed, or before an amputation, as a pain reliever. Sometimes it was also poured on the wound as an antiseptic. Since penicillin was not commonly used in medical treatment until 1945 (wikipedia.org/wiki/Penicillin#discovery), home remedies containing alcohol were quite common, even in homes where alcohol was not used as a beverage. When penicillin was available through doctors and hospitals, folks who couldn't afford the drug still used liquor, as it was multi-purpose. Alcohol is a common ingredient of cough syrups, mouthwashes and other over-the-counter products sold in our country today.

Hot tea with honey and lemon is a common cold remedy. I've used it for myself, my children and my grandchildren, without alcohol, always with decaffeinated tea. Sometimes for myself, I have added some spirits.

Prohibition turned some religious folks off from the use of any alcohol, medicinal or otherwise. However, alcohol was not as dangerous as some other products on the market.

In 1815 (snopes.com/cokelore/cocaine.asp)

> "Coca-Cola was named for its two 'medicinal' ingredients: extract of coca leaves and kola nuts. Just how much cocaine was originally in the formulation is hard to determine, but the drink undeniably contained some cocaine in its early days."

"Coca-Cola didn't become completely cocaine-free until 1929." Thus prohibition of alcohol, from 1920-1932, didn't cure the troubles of a society's addiction problems.

Even though there is no cocaine in today's Coca-Cola, it never ceases to amaze me how some hypocritical folks can condemn a person for drinking alcoholic beverages, yet think it's less sinful or harmful for them to use caffeine in their morning coffee, a cup of tea, or chocolate or some type of soda with or without a meal. (Why didn't the Prohibitionists try to prohibit addictive products other than alcohol?)

Some of the previously described fruit syrups and moonshine combinations, with or without whipped cream, are used over adult desserts, such as homemade ice cream, apple pie or bread pudding. Because of the alcohol, they are not usually used in recipes for children's treats.

Another of my family favorites is hard strawberry lemonade. I made this one up myself as a way to use up some frozen strawberries that were taking up too much of my freezer space. Squeeze four to six whole lemons into a gallon pitcher. Slice the lemons and add them to the juice along with one quart of water. Puree two quarts of strawberries in a blender. They can be either fresh or frozen. Use the lemon/water mixture to put enough liquid into the strawberries to blend them. I prefer frozen berries because no ice is needed to melt and water down the flavor. Add ½ to one full cup of moonshine (depending on the proof) or vodka (any amount desired); then stir. Fill the balance of the space in the pitcher with water; let stand around twenty minutes and stir again before serving. I like my strawberry lemonade tart, so don't add sugar, but it or Splenda can be added to the pitcher or to each glass to taste. The same recipe can be used with peaches or another fruit of choice. If one likes sugar, the frozen lemonade can be substituted for the real lemons, but you still need to add some water.

My daughter Malissa makes a wicked bananas Foster. She heats butter, brown sugar, rum (whisky or moonshine can be substituted) and vanilla extract into a pan and heats them for a few minutes while she slices bananas (around 4).

The bananas are dropped over a scoop or two of ice cream; then the hot sauce is poured over the combination. Walnuts or pecans sprinkled over the top make an extra-tasty treat. A recipe similar to hers can be found at: allrecipes.com/Recipe/bananas-foster-ii/Detail. aspx. (If one chooses to use rum, I suggest some of the fruit-flavored brands made in the Bahamas.)

Although I have never drunk a cup of coffee in my life and don't even like to smell the stuff, I can remember Grandma (and others) occasionally drinking what she called "Irish Coffee". Wikipedia describes it as a home remedy similar in mixture and use as a hot toddy. There are various ways to make Irish Coffee, or as the Blue Ridge mountain folks called it, "coffee lace". To make coffee lace, one first brews the coffee and pours it into a cup. A shot of moonshine, or legal whisky, is added to the coffee. Sugar and cream are added to taste. To make Irish Coffee, cream is a necessity. Originally (according to Blue Ridge) regular cream was added, but now in the days of expensive lattes, mochas, frappuccinos, and other classy coffee drinks, whipped cream is often added instead of regular cream.

There are also beverage recipes containing cocoa and tea, instead of coffee, with various other ingredients added, such as liquor and fruit syrups, whipped cream, mint, etc. It's fairly easy to come up with a variety of tasteful drinks and desserts with a few pantry items and a little use of the imagination.

By mixing with other things, a little moonshine can go a looooong way!

Aside from all the moonshining that went on in my family, neighborhood and in Appalachia, there were plenty of other homemade alcoholic beverages. My dad made hundreds of bottles of beer, or home brew, each year, but not to sell. Uncle Ed made wine. However, I did not get their recipes. In sharing this with a friend, Paula Penotte Kitts, she told me her dad not only made wine in their basement, but also wrote a book of his family's recipes.

Dr. Paul A. Penotte, a chiropractor in Ironton, Ohio, when I was a child wrote *A Folio of Home-made Wines* (1958). His daughters shared several of the recipes with me for this book. Two of my favorite flavors are dandelion and blackberry. They are included for your enjoyment. The following are direct quotes from his book:

> "NOTE: It is recommended that you investigate local, state and federal laws concerning manufacture of wine for personal use as pertains to your particular locality before experimenting with these recipes."

> "Among the wines that might be called specialties, is Dandelion wine. The flavor and after-taste [sic] of good Dandelion wine is quite delightful. It is best to pick the flowers early in the morning, just after they have opened for the first time. As a labor saving hint - a few ten-cent pieces distributed among a group of children can easily yield a bushel basket of dandelion blossoms in a short time. Of the two recipes which follow, the first produces a tart light wine, and the second a sweeter, heavier bodied [sic] wine.

DANDELION WINE # 1:

    2 qts. Flowers
    4 qts. boiling water
    3 lb. granulated sugar
    1 cake yeast
    4 lemons
    2 oranges

Cover flowers with boiling water. Let stand 36 hours. Strain and add sugar and juice of fruit. Stand 24 hours. Add yeast. When scum rises add beaten white of one egg. Stand three days, strain and bottle.

DANDELION WINE # 2:

    1 qt. blossoms
    1 gal. boiling water
    2 lb. sugar per gallon
    6 lemons to 10 gal.
    6 oranges to 10 gal.
    6 lb. raisins to 10 gal.
    1 cake yeast to 10 gal.

Best to make at least 10 gallon. Pour boiling water over blossoms. Add ½ total of sugar. Ferment 14 days. Strain. Add other half of sugar, juice of fruit and raisins. Add yeast. Stand 14 days, strain off and bottle."

Dr. Penotte's recipe for blackberry wine is:

"Measure the berries and bruise them. To every gallon add one quart of boiling water. Let mixture stand twenty-four hours stirring occasionally. Strain off the liquid into a cask and to every gallon add two pounds of sugar. Cork tight and let stand about one year and you will have wine fit for the finest table."

There are numerous recipes online for making wine and beer. Kits for production are also available for purchase at reasonable prices.

Now I must add an interesting story with some words of caution.

Many of the distillers mentioned in this publication were wonderful people and I knew them well, visited their homes, played with either them or their children and could vouch for the sanitation and safety of their products.

My father was a wonderful man. During my senior year of high school he accepted Christ into his life and heart and was truly a changed man. He attended church nearly every evening. He always knew where there was a songfest, a revival, a homecoming, retreat, Bible study, or some other form of spiritual feeding. When in the car, he listened to preachers and singers on the radio. He wanted every child in Bible school and Sunday school and furnished transportation to many. He totally stopped using alcohol in any form and made use of his extended illness as an opportunity to witness to others. He wanted Mom and/or one or more of his children with him at all times. He was as honest as anyone you could ever hope to find in this life on earth and the thought of ever committing a crime never entered his mind. He was particular about his appearance, nutrition and sanitation.

We moved to Ironton in the summer of 1963, following the completion of my sophomore year at Rock Hill High School. Except for a short period of time my brother Ronnie lived in our house at Kitts Hill upon his return from Vietnam, it was used only for our recreation. We kept pets there - a goat, a rabbit, chickens, cats, a mule, and some horses - because they could roam about and not need the constant care our recently sold dairy cattle had required. We still grew a garden on the property and there was plenty of food and water available for the animals. We took our dogs to town with us, but went out into the country almost every evening and weekend to let them roam and to ride our horses and to enjoy and care for the other pets.

Janet and I went away to college and Billy was seriously injured in a motorcycle accident. Ronnie was married, had a child and was busy with a job and a family. Mom and Dad were occupied at first visiting Billy at the hospital, as he was there for many months, and Shirley was busy with school and playing with new friends in the neighborhood.

Because we weren't using the farmhouse much, an old fellow and his wife asked Dad if they could rent it. (Dad never told me their names.) Although he didn't know the couple very well, he agreed because he thought the extra money would come in handy. The old fellow offered to take care of our pets. Dad assumed the man meant he would make sure the pets were fed and watered, which was not much of a task, but nice of him to offer. So, Dad agreed.

As Billy's condition improved, Dad decided to spend an afternoon alone, go to his farm, and ride his horse. When he got there the old folks were nowhere to be seen, nor was Rastus the goat, Bunny the rabbit, four farm cats or any one of the dozen chickens. As Dad drove past the house toward the barn, he noticed the carcass of the goat. It had been slaughtered and butchered. He deduced the same had probably happened to the rabbit and the chickens. He began to wonder about the horses, as his fatherly instincts took over and he tried to comprehend what the grief of losing so many pets at one time would do to his children, as we all were fond of our animals. Dad knew we'd have a period of grieving. As a new Christian our father was developing better ways to deal with such situations and his anger.

Dad told me he thought the old couple didn't get enough of a pension to live on and figured they ate the animals because they needed the food. Perhaps, he thought, when they told him they would take care of the animals, they meant "taking care of them" differently than he assumed. As he walked toward the outhouse, he saw the horses running down the steep hill to get to him. They were accustomed to plenty of attention and Dad was pleased to see they were safe and well.

When he opened the toilet door, he was shocked at what he saw. The old folks had set up a still in the smelly outhouse. Dad wanted no part of anything illegal on his property. He knew John and Minnie Scott were not living on their property when they were arrested, even though it was their still. But more than the fear of being arrested and charged for something he didn't do, Dad was repulsed by the thoughts of distilling anything in an outhouse.

No matter how clean and sanitary an outhouse was, it still smelled like shit and was swarmed by flies. Varmint droppings from possums and coons, animals that would even eat human waste, were observed. Dad became nauseated with the idea of distilling a beverage of any kind for human consumption in such an environment. Then he began to consider the danger of an explosion or the untended fire under the still spreading over his land and destroying the buildings, horses, crops and timber.

He calmed down a little with the warm greeting from his equine friends, saddled them up one at a time and rode them for a few hours until the old couple arrived. By that time, he had made up his mind what he'd do.

The above photo is of Dad on a filly in front of our house at Kitts Hill around 1963. His 1957 Ford is partially visible behind the horse.

When the elderly couple approached Dad they were staggering around, talking with slurred speech and carrying empty jugs. He questioned them about the goat, the rabbit and the chickens. They told him they had eaten all of them and those strange meowing squirrels as well.

Daddy told me he talked to them in a calm voice while trying to contain his temper, but gave them orders to move immediately.

Dad talked with me about the situation in detail when I came home for a visit. We went out to the farm to ride the horses and to the hospital to visit Billy.

Eating a goat, a rabbit and chickens was not as disturbing to Dad as eating the cats. He just could not get over them being so drunk that they actually ate those cats.

It was quite obvious to me that Dad found having a still in the outhouse totally repulsive. He had a discussion with me about never eating food from anyone's kitchen I had not inspected for a preview of cleanliness myself or never consuming any homemade food or drinks from strangers anywhere.

To this day, I rarely attend a potluck of any kind and if I do, I make sure not to eat anything from a kitchen I've never been in, unless it is one I know to be government-inspected. Then there are some places I won't eat if I have any suspicion of an owner or an employee not being "clean".

At the time Dad told me all this, it was a serious matter. Today as I am writing it, I can't help but smile as I share Dad's advice. The old couple he put "on the go" were not what one would consider the typical cook or chemist. They have been dead for many years now, but their kind do exist. Hopefully, you or I won't run across any like them.

So, to make a long story short, check out your cooks and chemists and be careful where you get your homemade wine, food or moonshine!

This page is intentionally blank.

Conclusion

I am truly grateful to all who encouraged me to write this book. It has been a wonderful learning experience because of the true spirit of community cooperation. The research has been extensive and time-consuming, but also very rewarding. I have been inspired from the love and laughter expressed in the voices of those who shared their anecdotal memories.

Hopefully you have enjoyed learning from this minute piece of recorded history.

When I ran across a snag or couldn't find a specific piece of information, I called upon friends, schoolmates, childhood neighbors and family. The memories of Norman Humphrey, Harley Vanmeter, Wayne Rucker, and Martha Kimble Yates have proven phenomenal. This book could not have been written without their assistance.

It is amazing how stories told to me by one person were verified by conversations with another, no matter the age of the individual providing the information. The stories also coincided with newspaper articles, court records and other bibliographical references, with the only exception being a discrepancy in information from two cousins. In that particular instance, I can't help but wonder how much has been kept from every child by a concerned parent or grandparent for the protection of that child's self/family image or memories of honor and respect for the deceased. However, children do grow up and seek the truth.

Not only have numerous people been cooperative in sharing oral information, many have provided photographs and newspaper articles as well. Most of us are proud of our ancestors. We realize how much they sacrificed for us and for future generations and how difficult it was for them to survive the worst depression in our nation's history.

I have not tried to tell everyone's story, but have used those stories provided voluntarily or from newspaper articles and court records to aid in developing an understanding of a general area within our county and our culture throughout the twentieth century.

Only one elderly lady would not discuss her family's participation in the illicit manufacturing of spirits with me. She did not deny the participation, but expressed to me she did not feel it was anything to be proud of, not anything to even be discussed. Yet prior to my contacting her, other members of her family volunteered some of the details without my asking. Although being respectful of the woman's age and feelings, I am thankful everyone does not have her personal views of family, truth, community and culture. At her request, I did not use her family's story in this publication. One family's unpublished story does not change the impact of the many others herein.

As far as honesty goes for adults, I don't believe it is completely honest to withhold the truth. Sometimes it is actually dishonest to not tell the whole truth.

Often we fail to realize everything we do, no matter what others think, is a part of our family, community, and national history.

I know I am not perfect. Other than Jesus Christ, on this earth no one has ever been or ever will be. We should not delude our children into thinking any one of us is.

In all of my imperfections, I am proud to be an American. I am thankful to have grown up in Lawrence County, Ohio, in our loving, but self-sufficient culture. I honor my parents and ancestors and hope sharing this part of our culture with you makes you think more of not just your ancestors, but of the historical picture we are currently painting for future generations. The least we can do is tell them the truth.

Perhaps some of us could benefit from hearing a sermon or two on John 8:32, "And you shall know the truth, and the truth shall make you free."

Again, as stated in my *Appalachian Childhood*, I believe,
> "All role models are good, even if
> their behaviors are not. It's all in how
> we use what we learn from their charac-
> teristics and how we set our minds to keep
> on learning and improving."

Moonshining and bootlegging are a celebrated part of our culture. That is a fact. Although numerous names of manufacturers (well over one hundred) were mentioned in this publication, there were many more (even within my own family) who were not, mainly because of the vast numbers of them and the time and financial aspects involved in locating newspaper articles, court records, and contacting family members for their views and memories.

The moonshiners mentioned herein were good people. Even those who were convicted and served prison sentences, when released lived crime-free lives once the nation's economy improved. (The only noted exception was Evans Barnett.) They were hardworking individuals who did what they had to do to survive and take care of their families. More importantly, they were loved and this love has tendered a legacy of good memories for their descendants and has inspired a celebrated part of our Appalachian history and culture.

May God bless you with a loving family, the strength to share His Eternal Love and a long life of happy experiences with good memories to share.

Bibliography

absoluteastronomy.com/discussionpost/ls_there_a_water_ heating_element_that_can_be used instead...

Advocate, The. Newark, Ohio. September 21, 1962.

Alcohol Fuel Producers Permit Under 26 U.S.C. 5181, March 13, 2001 (photographed by Marilyn Thornton Schraff) May 28, 2011.

allrecipes.com/recipe/bananas-foster-ii/detail.aspx

amazon.com/Moonshine-Drinking-Historical-Knee-Slappers-Recovering

ancestry.com

answers.com/topic/steam-still

Bates, Loraine. National Archives and Records Administration . Letter to Marilyn Schraff. March 21, 2011.

Benjamin, Cassandra. United States Department of Justice, Federal Bureau of Prisons. Letter to Marilyn Schraff. March 2, 2011.

blueridgeinstitute.org/moonshine/common_blue_ridge_ moonshining_terms.htm blueridgeinstitute.org/moonshine/still20_types_and_techniques.htm

blueridgeinstitute.org/moonshine/1980's_mash_recipe_for_corn_liquor.html

Bogzevits, Chris and John Winnenberg. *Our Journey Continues: The History of New Straitsville, Ohio. Volume 2: 1925-1950.* The New Straitsville Betterment Association & Sunday Creek Associates. New Straitsville, Ohio. U.S.A. 1996.

"Bootleg Days of Wet Capital of Ohio". (photographed by Marilyn Thornton Schraff) May 28, 2011.

campbellchapel.org/churchhistory.htm

Common Pleas Court of Lawrence County, Ohio. Cora Yates Plantiff. January 4, 1926.

Common Pleas Court of Lawrence County, Ohio. Case 16349. Cora Yates vs. Walter Neal Yates. Pages 564-566. Term 1926.

cooks.com/rec/doc/00,1823,145176-242206,00.htm

cooks.com/rec/doc/view/0,1932,139160-236200,00.html

cooks.com/rec/view/0,1723,149140-249199,00.htm

cooks.com/rec/view/0,173,151172-22407,00.html

Coshocton Tribune, The. Two Bandits Hunted Following Gun Battle In Which Three Are Killed; Name of Local Police Officer Found in Bandit's Notebook; Reason for Entry Is Mystery. Vol. XXIX, No. 13. Coshocton, Ohio. September 4, 1927. Page 2.

drinknation.com/drinkapple_pie_bulk

edocket.access.gpo.gov/efr_2006/aprgtr/27cfr24.75.htm

ehow.com (use the search and type in apple pie drink)

Encyclopedia of Appalachia. Abramson, Rudy and Haskell, Jean; The University of Tennessee Press/ Knoxville, U.S.A. First Edition. 2006.

ehow.com/how4703180_hot-toddy-recipe.html

en.wikipedia.org/wiki/Eighteenth_Amendment_to_the_United_States_Constitution

en.wikipedia.org/wiki/Irish-coffee

en.wikipedia.org/wiki/New_Straitsville,_Ohio

en.wikipedia.org/wiki/Van_Leer,_Kentucky

google.com/ whisky price history in google.com/whiskey price history in the States

http:www.whiskeywise.com/Moonshine-Whiskey.html Illegal Whiskey produced in the USA

Highway Map of Lawrence County Ohio. Lind, David R. P.E. and P.S. County Engineer. 2006-2007.

Holy Bible, King James Version, The Scofield Study Bible, Oxford Press, New York. U.S.A. 2003.

homedistiller.org/image/mini_explained.jpg

Honor Roll of Lawrence County Ohio, World War I Soldiers. Miller, Ernest. Ironton, Ohio. 1919.

hyperhistory.com

Ironton City Directory. 1883-84. Ironton, Ohio, U.S.A.

Ironton City Directory. 1938. Ironton, Ohio, U.S.A.

Ironton City Directory. 1939. Ironton, Ohio, U.S.A.

Ironton Evening Tribune. Mae Davis, Evans Barnett Double Murder Victims. Friday June 25, 1937. Page 1.

Ironton Tribune. 26 Persons Named Co-Conspirators In Liquor Ring, Lawrence County People Alleged To Be Implicated With Officers, Proctorville Marshal and Deputy to Be Tried May 25. March 29, 1932. Page 2.

Ironton Tribune. Carson and Neff Plead Not Guilty; Bond Set at $10,000. May 5, 1932. Page 8.

Ironton Tribune. Enormous Still. (no date, but sometime during Prohibition).

Ironton Tribune. Federal Grand Jury Indicts Neff, Carson. April, 11, 1932. Page 6.

Ironton Tribune. Homer Delawder Killed. August 3, 1931. Page 1.

Ironton Tribune. Merry-Making At Murder Scene Short Time Before Series of Shots Heard. June 1937.

Ironton Tribune. More Than 40 Persons Indicted. April 16, 1932. Page 2.

Ironton Tribune. Officials Seek Identity of Mystery Car Occupants. June 26, 1937. Page 1.

Ironton Tribune. Scioto and Lawrence Liquor Ring. October 29, 1939.

Ironton Tribune. The Church That Tom Built, First Anniversary of Church Easter. (no exact date, about Spring of 1959).

Ironton Evening Tribune. Was Killed In Auto Accident. October 23, 1926.

Koskoff, David E. *Joseph P. Kennedy A Life and Times.* 1974. Prentice-Hall, Inc. Englewood Cliffs, New Jersey. Pages 51-53.

Lawrence County Ohio Auditor's Office, Deed 122-363. Walter Neal Yates to Cora A. Yates. August 25, 1925.

Logan Daily News. Michal and Video Florida Bound. February 28, 1989.

manta.com/c/mm29673/scott-chemical-co

mapquest.com

Marion Star, The. Dies in Fire Near Ashley. Marion, Ohio. January 25, 1940.

Marion Star, The. Elder Dingledine Caught, Returned to Springfield, Suspect in Holdup Slayings Yields Meekly To Face First Degree Murder Charge; Denies Part in Killings. Marion, Ohio. September 27, 1937. Page 2.

Merriam-Webster Unabridged Dictionary. Authority and Inn, Incorporated CD Version 2.5. 2000.

Mitchum, Robert. *Thunder Road*. 1958. Metro Goldwyn Mayer. Sony Home Entertainment. Culver City, California. 1958.

moonshiners.com/uploads/reunion.asp

ofea.org/view.php?fest_id-r Ohio Festivals & Events Association

Ohio Festivals and Events Association Brochure.

ohiohistorycentral.org/entry.php?rec=544&nm-Prohibition

Owl, The 1965. Ironton High School Yearbook. Ironton, Ohio. 1965. Page 64.

Penotte, Paul A. *A Folio of Home-Made Wines*. 1958. Ironton, Ohio.

Portsmouth Daily Times, The. Taken to U. S. Court. October 23, 1923. Page 3.

Prohibition.osu.edu/content/

Schraff, Marilyn Thornton. *Appalachian Childhood: Memories of Growing Up In Rural Southern Ohio During The Mid 20th Century*. 2010. Marilyn Thornton Schraff, Cleveland, Ohio, U.S.A. Page 125.

Schwarz, Ted. *Joseph P. Kennedy The Mogul, The Mob, The Statesman And The Making Of An American Myth* 2003. John Wiley & Sons Inc. Hoboken, New Jersey. Pages 95- 96.

Shakespeare, William. Romeo and Juliet. London, England. (1600's).

snopes.com/cokelore/cocaine.asp

State of Ohio, Delaware County Probate Court Affadavit 11091, Charging Paul Legg. September 26, 1926.

State of Ohio, Delaware County Probate Court Arraignment of Paul Legg. September 28, 1926.

State of Ohio, Delaware County Probate Court Recognizance for Paul Legg by Lee Main. September 30, 1926.

State of Ohio, Delaware County Probate Court Warrant to Arrest Paul Legg, September 27, 1926.

Stewart, Bruce E. *Moonshiners and Prohibitionists,* The University Press of Kentucky, U.S.A. 2011.

Thacker, Donald. E-letter to Marilyn Schraff. Recipe. February 25, 2011.

thesunsfinancialdiary.com/poll/federal-minimum-wage-725hour-chart-day/ Federal Minimum Wage

Time Recorder, The. Acquitted on One Charge Arrested on Another. Zanesville, Ohio. October 6, 1933.

Time Recorder, The. Father, Son and Friend Die in Electric Chair For Murder of Peace Officers. Zanesville, Ohio. Volume LV, No. 93. Page 1.

ttb.gov.beer.25_205_.htm/Sec.25.205production

ttb.gov. Department of the Treasury Alcohol and Tobacco Tax and Trade Bureau Statistical Report-Distilled Spirit, March 2, 2011

ttb.fags/genalcohol.shtml

ttb.gov/statistics/95newsa08.htm. Illicit Liquor (MOONSHINE) Page A-8.

ttb.treas.gov History of ATF

War Ration Book No. 3. United States of America Office of Price Administration Form No. R-130. U.S Government Printing Office: 1943.

wikionary. revenuer

wikipedia.org/wiki/Penicillin#discovery

United States District Court Southern District of Ohio Western Division Indictment, case number 5555, October 21, 1939 to November 1, 1939.

Yates, Walter Neal. Personal Diary. (unpublished) 1902-1942.

Family Business

Federal agents
liquor banned
arrested Grandma
searched her land

Chased her brothers
firing guns
prison time
served three sons

Illicit spirits
in the hills
homemade whisky
copper stills

Carefully cooked
blended fine
country chemists
made moonshine

Marilyn Thornton Schraff
August 19, 2011

Index of Persons

Abner, Clarence, 123
Adams, Robert, 38
Adams, Virgil, 38
Akers, Kathy Delawder, ix, 53, 56
Arnold, Robert L, 123
Ball, James S., 123
Barnett, Evans, 45, 48-50, 52, 79, 183
Barnett, Rufus, 45, 47
Birchfield, Bob, ix, 133
Birchfield, Robert, 72, 132
Birchfield, Sadie, 72, 132
Blankenship, Bill, 125
Blankenship, David, ix, 125, 141
Boggs, Phillip, 113
Boggs, Squire, 49
Bowen, John, 123
Bowen, Oscar S., 123
Bowman, Maxine Bennett, ix
Bragg, Herman W., 123
Brown, Rema, 7, 11
Burgess, Kenny, 7, 11
Butler, Bonnie, 7, 11
Caldwell, Michael, ix, 35
Capone, Al, 30

Carmon, David, 84, 86
Carson, Orville, 78
Carter, Fred, 48
Chapman, Harry, 50
Chapman, Jennifer, ix, 124
Childers, Mabel, 70
Christ, Jesus, xv, 28, 90-91, 124, 174, 182
Christian, Phyllis Humphrey, ix
Clark, Stanley, 123
Clary, Phyllis Waugh, ix, 114
Coach, Revenuer or Agent, 56, 57, 76, 91-95, 124-125
Coleman, Bernice, 37
Collins, Lafe B., 123
Collins, Lee, 123
Collins, Oakley, 132
Comer, Shirley Thornton, 10, 23, 82, 175
Conway, Lonnie, 58
Cotton, Charles, 37
Crisp, Robert, 38
Cunningham, Thomas, 123
Dalton, Forest, 34, 35
Davis, Ron, ix, 132
Delawder, Albert, 45- 47, 51- 53, 56, 58, 69, 72, 111-112, 114, 116,122,

Delawder, Amos, 46, 52-53, 69
Delawder, Bill, 47
Delawder, Clarence, 53, 67-68
Delawder, Dorothy, 47
Delawder, Ernest, 46, 52-53, 67-68, 70
Delawder, Hobart, 20, 46, 53, 57, 65-67, 69, 75, 103-104, 106-107, 116, 119, 121
Delawder, Homer, 52-53, 56, 67-72, 110, 116, 122, 132
Delawder, John, ix, 46, 53, 69, 100, 110
Delawder, Joseph, 13, 43, 46, 53
Delawder, Kenneth, 47
Delawder, Lona, 67-68, 71
Delawder, Lydia Neal, 13-14, 46, 53, 111
Delong, Ann (Yates), 43
Delong, James, ix
Delong, Marcella Dickess, ix
Delong, Raymond, 45, 97, 101-102, 106-107, 111, 117
Delong, Robert, 45
Delong, Thomas, 38, 40, 43, 45, 97, 100-104, 106-107, 110-111, 117
Dement, Sheriff, 45
Dingledines (see below)
Dingledine, Harry, 49, 50
Dingledine, Henry, 49, 50
Doyle, Cora Yates, ix, 61
Drake, John, 139
Duncan, Don, 123
Dunfee, Ben, 78
Eaches, Sharon Sites, 134
Elkins, Prosecutor, 46, 78
Eubanks, Lyndall Murdock, ix, 142
Evicks, Garnett, 62
Feuillerat, June, ix
Fox, Judy, iv, x
Fradd Betty, ix, 132
Fradd, Earl, 131, 132
Fraley, Betty Moore, ix
Fuller, Kenneth, 123
Gayle, Crystal, 59
Gillette, Turley, 123
Glenn, William, 74
Greene, Dan & Randy, 84
Griffith, Earl, 35
Griffith, Fred, 36, 72
Gullett, Blaine, 38
Haas, Patrolman, 36
Hamilton, Morris, 38
Hampton, Albert, 123
Hankins, Dennis, 134
Harper, Alvin, 45
Harper, Lawrence, 111
Hawk, Fred, 152

Hayes, John, 38
Hennington, Elmer, 123
Henson, Carl, 123
Hieronimus, Daniel, ix, 83, 86, 87
Holderby, James, 123
Holderman, Herman, 123
Howard, Margaret, 70
Hugger, George, 36
Humphrey, Norman, ix, 53-54, 57, 59-60, 76, 94-95, 116, 121, 181
Hunter, Doc, 93
Jayne, Charles, 134
Jenkins, Betty, ix
Jenkins, Fred, 123
Jenkins, Homer Eugene, ix
Jenkins, Ruth, 129
Jenkins, Thomas, 128-130, 136, 142
Jennings, Waylon, 133
Johnson, LeRoy, 123
Johnson, Paul, ix, 97, 108, 116, 119, 121
Johnson, Ricky, ix, 120
Johnson, Ronald Bruce, 10
Jones, Allen, 38
Jones, Bill, 38
Jones, John (Jack), 84-85
Jones, Loomis, 123
Jones, Stella, 37

Kamer, Elizabeth, 123
Keeney, Alma & Thomas, 110
Keeney, Amos, 101
Keeney, C.H., 100
Kelly, James Thomas, 74, 113, 117
Kelly, Nola Rucker, 116-117
Kelly, Thomas G., 97, 104, 106-107, 116-117, 122
Kelly, Wayne, 68, 70, 118
Kemper, Rev., 69
Kempner, Rev., 51
Kennedy, Joseph, 30-31
Kersey, Lori, ix
Kimble, Bernard Russell, 123
Kitts, Danny, ix, 125
Kitts, Paula Penotte, ix, 146, 172
Koskoff, David, 30-31
Lambert, Donald, ix, 120
Lambert, Randall, ix
Lambert, Steven, ix
Leeper, Patricia Yates, ix, 41-42
Leffingwell, Nettie, 47, 114
Legg, Charles, ix, 109
Legg Paul, 97-105, 107, 109, 115, 118, 121-122
Lewis, Hazel, 62
Lewis, Mae Davis, 48-50

Liggins, Wilson, 38
Lightner, Sharon, ix
Little, Dianna Yates, ix, 62
Lloyd, William, 37
Locey, Gerard, 142
Loper, Bessie B., 48
Lynn, Loretta, 59
Maghni, Jesse, 37
Main, Arthur, ix
Main, Jonah, 71, 74, 100, 109, 121
Main, Lee, 109-110, 121-122
Malone, Dorothy, ix
Malone, George, ix
Mart, Nellie, 47
Massie, Charles (Butch), ix, 129, 136, 156
Matney, Floyd, 58
Mays, Willard, 34-35
McClure, George, 54
McDowell, Ray, 51
McIntyre, Emmett, ix, 84
McKee, Lewis, 84-85
McKee, Marie, 70, 84
McKnight, Danny, ix
McLoughlin, Mack, 123
Miller, Andrew Jackson, 126, 132
Miller, Fletcher, 126-127
Miller, Helen Delawder, 53, 67, 69, 126, 132
Miller, Lenora, ix, 53, 69-70, 72
Miller, Magnolia Adkins, 126
Mills, Olan (photographic studio), ix, 3
Moore, Ambrose, 68, 70-71, 121
Moore, Edgar, 70-71
Moore, Edith, 70
Murdock, Donna, 142
Murdock, Lowell, 142-143
Murdock, Lyndall, ix, 142
Murdock, Vivian, 142
Murray, Hugh, 110
Neal, George, 34-35
Neal, Lydia (see Delawder)
Neff, Meldon, 78
Pearson, Garland, 37
Pendleton, Jesse, 38
Penotte, Paul, 172-173
Peters, Turkey, 36
Phillips, Mortician (Undertaker), 51, 69
Pinkerman, Jim, 72, 93, 124-125, 133, 135
Ramey, Marta Sutton, ix, 88, 110-111
Ratliff, Carl, ix, 141
Ratliff, Mavis Siders, ix, 141
Riffitt, John, 36
Riley, Albert T., 127-128
Roach, Joyce Hardy, ix
Roberts, John William (Bill), 72, 134-136 (Ruth, 135)
Robinson, Willis, 37
Rose, Carl, 139

Ross. F.R., 36
Rucker, Joe, 43, 116
Rucker, Uriah (Babe), 43
Rucker, Wayne, ix, 49, 181
Russell, Ben, 37
Sanders, George, ix, 125
Scherer, Anita Sanders, ix, 133, 135
Schwarz, Ted, 30
Scott, Elwood, 139
Scott, George, ix, 139
Scott, John, 133, 139-141, 176
Scott, Minnie, 133, 139-141, 176
Searls, Kaitlyn, 128
Searls, Michal Thompson, iv, vii, ix, 1-12, 21-22, 24, 152
Searls, Noel, 127
Searls, Ronald, ix, 127
Shafer, Lori, ix
Shakespeare, William, 77
Shope, Charles, 36
Siders, John & Frances, 141
Siders, Marvin, 97, 100, 108, 110, 116, 119, 141
Smith, Augusta, 123
Smith, Carl Lloyd, 136-137, 149, 153, 157, 161
Smith, John, 123
Smith, Larry, 124
Smith, Leroy, 123
Smith, Oscar, 123
Smith, Otho, 123
Smith, Stanford, 123
Sowards, Jacob, 123
Spears, Brenda Moore, ix
Sprouse, Bill, 72, 137-138, 149, 161-163, 167
Sprouse, Don, 72, 137-138, 149, 161-163
Sprouse, Proctor, 137-138, 149, 161-163
Sprouse, Ted, ix, 137-139, 149, 162
Stapleton, Bill, 139
Steed, Charles, 103, 116
Stone, Abberman, 38
Strehle, Yvonne, ix, 61
Thacker, Donald, ix, 145
Thomas, Cora W., ix, 120
Thomas, Ronald, ix, 134
Thomas, Viola Adkins, ix
Thompson, Malissa (Nazir), vii, ix, 1-6, 21-22, 25, 63, 152, 170
Thornton, Billy, 113, 175, 178
Thornton, Janet, 2, 23, 175
Thornton, Marilyn, 2, 23
Thornton, Martin T., 13, 70
Thornton, Mary, 166

Thornton, Ray, 34, 82-83
Thornton, Ronnie, 70-71, 113, 136, 139, 141, 175
Thornton, Vedna Yates (Mom), 10-12, 15-16, 18, 20-22, 57, 63, 65, 71, 82, 114, 117, 121, 167-168, 174-175 (also known as Vedna Harmon)
Thornton, William L. (Dad), 21, 64, 112 174-178
Tufts, Loraine C., 145
Uhl, Jerry, iv, ix, 8, 24-25
Vanmeter, Harley, x, 50, 109, 181
Volgares, Gladys Miller, 126
Volgares, James, x, 126
Walden, Evan, x
Walls, Betty Jenkins, x, 128
Washington, Andrew, 88
Washington, George, 28
Waugh, Cora, 93
Waugh, Ernest, 62
Waugh, Gene, x, 120, 163
Waugh, George, x, 120, 163
Waugh, Harlan (Harlin), 97, 102-104, 106-107, 114-118, 120
Waugh, Ida, 41, 72, 114, 120
Waugh, Johnny, 93-94, 120
Waugh, Lem, 92, 94, 120
Waugh, Otis, 94, 120
Waugh, Willard, 97, 108, 114-116, 119-120, 163
Webb, L. Gail Neal, x, 35
Weber, Bonnie (McGoron), x
Wellman, James, 123
West, State Agent, 36
Wicker, Sandy, x
Wickline, David L., x
Wileman, City Patrolman, 36
Williams, Lou, 123
Williams, Peggy Penotte, x
Wilson, Mat, 45
Wilson, Mildred, x
Winters, William, x
Wopat, Tom, 7
Yates, Benjamin, 43
Yates, Charles, 54-55, 112
Yates, Cora Delawder, 13-15, 41, 46, 52-53, 56, 97, 100-101, 103-104, 106-107, 121
Yates, Earl, 15-16, 18, 41-42, 56-57, 68, 70, 97, 100-104, 106-107, 116-117, 121
Yates, Edna, 16, 18-20, 57
Yates, Forrest Ray, x, 62

Yates, Forrest Rose, 16, 43, 53, 56-57, 62-64, 71, 74, 96-97, 100-104, 106-107, 110, 113, 120, 149
Yates, Harold, x, 43, 93, 121
Yates, Isaac (Ike), 13, 15-16, 54, 57-62, 68, 70, 73-74, 92, 121
Yates, Joseph (Joe), 16-17, 42, 57
Yates, Marion, 15, 38, 40-44, 55, 57, 71, 74, 92, 97, 99-100, 102-105, 107, 110, 114, 116, 120-121, 133
Yates, Martha Kimble, x, 58-61, 117, 181
Yates, Nellie, 15
Yates, Paul, 37, 43
Yates, Paul David, 62
Yates, Polly Neal, 13
Yates, Sharon Dee, 61
Yates, Shirley Marie, 16
Yates, Tammy Shellene, 61
Yates, Walter Neal (Grandpa), 13-15, 19-20, 41, 52, 54-57, 70
Yates, Walter Richard, 62

Grandma as I remember her (late 1950s)

Index of Illustrations

1. My little princess and me — 2
2. Michal and Malissa Thompson — 3
3. Tom Wopat and Michal Thompson — 7
4. Michal at 16 as Miss Moonshine — 8
5. Michal by New Straitsville sign — 9
6. Shirley Comer, Vedna Thornton and Bruce Johnson — 10
7. Rema Brown, Bonnie Butler, Kenny Burgess and Michal Thompson — 11
8. A beautiful, happy Miss Moonshine — 12
9. Cora Delawder Yates and Walter Neal Yates — 14
10. Joseph Yates — 17
11. Milk can — 18
12. Edna Yates as a teen — 19
13. Vedna May Yates Thornton at age 17 — 22
14. Marilyn, Shirley and Janet Thornton — 23
15. Michal Thompson as a teen — 24
16. Malissa Thompson as a teen — 25
17. Blue Ration Stamps — 32
18. Red Ration Stamps — 33
19. Willard Mays, Forest Dalton and George Neal with a still — 35
20. Earl Yates, Justice of the Peace — 42
21. Marion Yates in WW II uniform in 1943 — 44
22. Some of the Delawder Brothers — 46
23. Charles Yates during WWI — 55
24. Floyd Matney, Lonnie Conway and Isaac Yates in 1932 — 58
25. Isaac Yates in WWII uniform — 60

26.	Isaac and Martha Kimble Yates	61
27.	Forrest Rose Yates during WW II	62
28.	Unknown, Forrest Yates and William L. Thornton	64
29.	Hobart Delawder	66
30.	Rock house cave	75
31.	Barn on Yates property	76
32.	Ray Thornton	83
33.	Lewis McKee	85
34.	John (Jack) S. Jones	85
35.	David Carmon	86
36.	Dan Hieronimus	86
37.	Highway Patrolman Hieronimus	87
38.	Sheriff Hieronimus	87
39.	Andrew Washington and others	88
40.	Bill Thornton at rock house cave	112
41.	Billy and Ronnie Thornton with Phillip Boggs	113
42.	Harlan Waugh in WW II uniform	114
43.	Willard Waugh	115
44.	Thomas G. Kelly in WW II uniform	117
45.	Cora Delawder Yates in 1937	118
46.	Fletcher Miller	127
47.	Thomas Jenkins as a young man	129
48.	Tom Jenkins in chauffeur's cap	130
49.	Earl Fradd	131
50.	Dennis Hankins	134
51.	Bill Roberts	136
52.	Carl Lloyd Smith	137
53.	Minnie Scott	140
54.	Front of still in parade	147
55.	Back of still in parade	148
56.	Moonshine Express in parade	148

57. Still at 2011 Moonshine Festival	151
58. Malissa Thompson, Fred Hawk and Michal Thompson	152
59. Drawing of still	156
60. Confiscated still	164
61. Bill Thornton and filly	177
62. Grandma in the late 1950's	202
63. *Appalachian Childhood* book front cover	206

Marilyn is also the author of ***Appalachian Childhood: Memories of Growing Up In Rural Southern Ohio During The Mid 20th Century***, a nonfiction book published in 2010.

Appalachian Childhood

Memories of Growing Up In Rural Southern Ohio During The Mid 20th Century

Marilyn Thornton Schraff

Mail Order Page
for
Appalachian Childhood

Customer name_____

Mailing Address:_____

_____

Telephone number:_____

Number of copies requested:_____

Price per book: $19.00 (nineteen dollars and no cents)

Sales tax rate: 7% or $1.33 per book

Shipping cost is an additional $3.95 (three dollars and ninety-five cents).

For further information call: 216-401-2192

Payment must be received prior to shipment.

Mail order form and check or money order to:

Marilyn Thornton Schraff
189 Summit Street
Marion, OH 43302-4207

Mail Order Page for
Moonshine

Customer name_____

Mailing Address:_____

_____

Telephone number:_____

Number of copies requested:_____

Price per book: $19.99 (nineteen dollars and ninety-nine cents)

Sales tax rate: 7% or $1.40 per book

Shipping cost is an additional $3.95 (three dollars and ninety-five cents).

For further information call: 216-401-2192

Payment must be received prior to shipment.

Mail order form and check or money order to:

Marilyn Thornton Schraff
189 Summit Street
Marion, OH 43302-4207